HESSEN ENTDECKEN

Schlösser · Burgen · Klöster · Gärten

DISCOVER HESSE

Palaces · Castles · Monasteries · Gardens

HESSEN ENTDECKEN

Schlösser · Burgen · Klöster · Gärten

DISCOVER HESSE

Palaces · Castles · Monasteries · Gardens

Mit Fotografien von Michael Leukel
With photographs by Michael Leukel

Katharina Bechler und Kirsten Worms (Hg.)
Published by Katharina Bechler and Kirsten Worms

Staatliche
Schlösser und Gärten
Hessen

MICHAEL IMHOF VERLAG

INHALT

Das kulturelle Erbe der Staatlichen Schlösser und Gärten Hessen –
eine Rundreise

10	**Grußwort** Volker Bouffier
12	**Zum Geleit** Angela Dorn
14	**Willkommen** Kirsten Worms
18	**Vorwort und Dank** Michael Leukel
20	**48 Kulturschätze auf einen Blick**

IM TAUNUS

26	Schloss und Schlosspark Bad Homburg, Bad Homburg vor der Höhe
32	Burgruine Oberreifenberg, Oberreifenberg
34	Burgruine Altweilnau, Weilrod-Altweilnau
36	Hutturm Walsdorf, Idstein-Walsdorf
38	Burgruine Hohenstein, Hohenstein
40	Burgruine Geroldstein, Heidenrod-Geroldstein

WEILBURG UND UMGEBUNG

44	Schloss und Schlossgarten Weilburg, Weilburg
50	Burgruine Merenberg, Merenberg

UNESCO-WELTERBE „GRENZEN DES RÖMISCHEN REICHES" IM TAUNUS

54	Römerkastell Kleiner Feldberg, Glashütten
56	Römerkastell Kapersburg, Rosbach vor der Höhe
58	Römerbrunnen Kaichen, Kaichen

WETTERAU, MARBURGER LAND UND VOGELSBERG

62	Fürstengruft Butzbach, Butzbach
64	Burgruine Münzenberg, Münzenberg
68	Adolfsturm und St. Georgsbrunnen, Burg Friedberg, Friedberg
70	Junker-Hansen-Turm, Neustadt
72	Elisabethbrunnen Schröck, Marburg-Schröck
74	Galgen von Hopfmannsfeld, Lautertal/Hopfmannsfeld

IM NORDEN HESSENS

78	Hafenbecken Bad Karlshafen, Bad Karlshafen
80	Schloss Spangenberg, Spangenberg
82	Burgruine Felsberg, Felsberg
84	Burg Fürsteneck, Eiterfeld

VON NORD NACH SÜD – KLÖSTER, KIRCHEN UND EINE KAISERPFALZ

88	Kloster Cornberg, Cornberg
90	Stiftsruine Bad Hersfeld, Bad Hersfeld
96	Propstei Johannesberg, Fulda
100	Kloster Konradsdorf, Ortenberg-Konradsdorf
102	Kaiserpfalz Gelnhausen, Gelnhausen
106	Kloster und Klostergarten Seligenstadt, Seligenstadt
112	Einhardsbasilika, Michelstadt-Steinbach
116	Kloster Lorsch, Lorsch, UNESCO-Welterbe

HANAU UND SEINE GRAFEN

124 Staatspark Hanau-Wilhelmsbad, Hanau
130 Schloss Steinau, Steinau a. d. Straße
134 Burg- und Schlossruine Schwarzenfels,
Sinntal-Schwarzenfels

DARMSTADT UND BERGSTRASSE

140 Prinz-Georg-Garten, Darmstadt
146 Fürstengruft Darmstadt, Darmstadt
148 Burgruine Frankenstein, Mühltal
150 Staatspark Fürstenlager, Bensheim-Auerbach
156 Schloss Auerbach, Bensheim-Auerbach

AM RHEIN

160 Schlosspark Biebrich, Wiesbaden
162 Brentano-Haus, Oestrich-Winkel
166 Zeppelindenkmal, Trebur-Geinsheim

UNESCO-WELTERBE OBERES MITTELRHEINTAL

170 Burgruine Ehrenfels, Rüdesheim am Rhein
172 Osteinscher Niederwald, Rüdesheim am
Rhein
178 Niederwalddenkmal, Rüdesheim am Rhein

VOM ODENWALD ZUM NECKAR

184 Schloss Erbach, Erbach
192 Schloss Lichtenberg, Fischbachtal-
Lichtenberg
196 Burg Breuberg, Breuberg
200 Veste Otzberg, Otzberg
202 Burg Hirschhorn, Hirschhorn

208 Impressum

CONTENTS

The Cultural Heritage of State Palaces and Gardens Hesse –
A Tour

10 **Preface** *Volker Bouffier*
12 **Foreword** *Angela Dorn*
14 **Welcome** *Kirsten Worms*
18 **Foreword and Acknowledgement**
   Michael Leukel
22 **48 Cultural Treasures at a Glance**

IN THE TAUNUS REGION

26 *Bad Homburg Palace and Palace Park,*
   Bad Homburg vor der Höhe
32 *Oberreifenberg Castle Ruins, Oberreifenberg*
34 *Altweilnau Castle Ruins, Weilrod-Altweilnau*
36 *Hutturm Tower Walsdorf, Idstein-Walsdorf*
38 *Hohenstein Castle Ruins, Hohenstein*
40 *Geroldstein Castle Ruins, Heidenrod-Geroldstein*

WEILBURG AND THE SURROUNDING AREA

44 *Weilburg Palace and Palace Gardens, Weilburg*
50 *Merenberg Castle Ruins, Merenberg*

UNESCO WORLD HERITAGE SITE "FRONTIERS
OF THE ROMAN EMPIRE" IN THE TAUNUS REGION

54 *Roman Fort of Kleiner Feldberg, Glashütten*
56 *Roman Fort of Kapersburg, Rosbach vor der*
   Höhe
58 *Roman Well Kaichen, Kaichen*

WETTERAU, MARBURGER LAND AND VOGELSBERG

62 *The Fürstengruft Princely Crypt Butzbach,*
   Butzbach
64 *Münzenberg Castle Ruins, Münzenberg*
68 *Adolf's Tower and the St George Fountain,*
   Friedberg Castle, Friedberg
70 *Junker-Hansen Tower, Neustadt*
72 *The Elisabeth Fountain, Schröck,*
   Marburg-Schröck
74 *The Gallows of Hopfmannsfeld,*
   Lautertal/Hopfmannsfeld

IN NORTH HESSE

78 *Bad Karlshafen Harbour Basin, Bad Karlshafen*
80 *Spangenberg Palace, Spangenberg*
82 *Felsberg Castle Ruins, Felsberg*
84 *Fürsteneck Castle, Eiterfeld*

FROM NORTH TO SOUTH – MONASTERIES,
CHURCHES AND AN IMPERIAL PALACE

88 *Cornberg Monastery, Cornberg*
90 *Bad Hersfeld Collegiate Church Ruins,*
   Bad Hersfeld
96 *Johannesberg Provostry Buildings, Fulda*
100 *Konradsdorf Monastery, Ortenberg-Konradsdorf*
102 *Imperial Palace of Gelnhausen, Gelnhausen*
106 *Seligenstadt Abbey and Abbey Garden,*
   Seligenstadt
112 *Einhard's Basilica, Michelstadt-Steinbach*
116 *Lorsch Abbey, Lorsch, UNESCO World Heritage*
   Site

HANAU AND ITS COUNTS

124 *Hanau-Wilhelmsbad State Park, Hanau*
130 *Steinau Palace, Steinau an der Straße*
134 *Schwarzenfels Castle and Palace Ruins,*
     Sinntal-Schwarzenfelsø

DARMSTADT AND THE MOUNTAIN ROAD

140 *Prince George Garden, Darmstadt*
146 *The Fürstengruft Princely Crypt Darmstadt,*
     Darmstadt
148 *Frankenstein Castle Ruins, Mühltal*
150 *Fürstenlager State Park, Bensheim-Auerbach*
156 *Auerbach Palace, Bensheim-Auerbach*

ON THE RIVER RHINE

160 *Biebrich Palace Park, Wiesbaden*
162 *Brentano House, Oestrich-Winkel*
166 *Zeppelin Monument, Trebur-Geinsheim*

UNESCO WORLD HERITAGE SITE "UPPER MIDDLE RHINE VALLEY"

170 *Ehrenfels Castle Ruins, Rüdesheim am Rhein*
172 *Ostein's Niederwald Park, Rüdesheim am Rhein*
178 *Niederwald Monument, Rüdesheim am Rhein*

FROM THE ODENWALD FOREST TO THE NECKAR RIVER

184 *Erbach Palace, Erbach*
192 *Lichtenberg Palace, Fischbachtal-Lichtenberg*
196 *Breuberg Castle, Breuberg*
200 *Otzberg Fortress, Otzberg*
202 *Hirschhorn Castle, Hirschhorn*

208 *Legal Notice*

GRUSSWORT

Hessen, seine Kunst und seine Kultur sind weltoffen, sie sind international und modern. In gleicher Weise sind Kunst und Kultur als historische Zeugnisse der Geschichte unseres Landes verpflichtet – einer langen Geschichte, die sich fortwährend im Austausch mit anderen Kulturen entwickelte, von denen Hessen neue Einflüsse aufgenommen und sich anverwandelt hat. Als kulturhistorisches Erbe unseres Landes erzählen seine Burgen, seine Schlösser und Gärten, seine Gebäude mit Geschichte von der Entwicklung eines ursprünglich in viele Territorien zersplitterten Landes und seinen Fürsten. Heute tragen diese Denkmäler zur Identität unseres demokratischen Landes bei und machen viele Orte unverwechselbar.

Fast 50 dieser Anlagen, angesiedelt in vielen Teilen des Landes, stehen unter der Obhut der Staatlichen Schlösser und Gärten. Herzlich gratuliere ich zum 75-jährigen Jubiläum. Seit der Errichtung der Institution trugen und tragen viele Menschen in verschiedenen Funktionen dazu bei, dieses Erbe durch Vermittlung, Erforschung, Schutz, Pflege und Präsentation zu bewahren. Dafür danke ich allen. Ich freue mich, wenn anlässlich des Jubiläums mit diesem Bildband ein Überblick über den Bestand der Staatlichen Schlösser und Gärten Hessen vorgelegt wird. Den Leserinnen und Lesern wünsche ich eine anregende Betrachtung und Lektüre.

Volker Bouffier
Hessischer Ministerpräsident

PREFACE

Hesse, its art and its culture are cosmopolitan, international and modern. At the same time, art and culture bear testimony to the history of our region. A long history, which developed continuously through interaction with other cultures that provided new influences for Hesse to assimilate. Hesse's castles, palaces, gardens and historical buildings represent our cultural heritage and tell the story of the development of a region, originally split into many territories, and its princes. Today, these monuments form part of the identity of our democratically constituted state and bestow a unique character on many localities. Almost 50 of these sites, spread throughout the region, are in the care of State Palaces and Gardens Hesse (Staatliche Schlösser und Gärten Hessen). I should like to congratulate the organisation on its 75th anniversary. Since its establishment, many people in many different roles have helped and continue to help to conserve this heritage through communication, research, protection, maintenance and presentation. I extend my thanks to all of you for this endeavour. I am delighted that this book, published to commemorate the anniversary, presents an overview of State Palaces and Gardens Hesse's portfolio and hope that readers will enjoy the fascinating images and information it contains.

Volker Bouffier
Minister-President of Hesse

ZUM GELEIT

Liebe Leserinnen und Leser,

vor Ihnen liegt ein besonderer Bildband: Alle 48 Burgen, Schlösser, Parks und Einzelmonumente im Besitz der Staatlichen Schlösser und Gärten Hessen sind in einem Werk vereint. Vom Staatspark Fürstenlager im Süden bis zum Hafenbecken Bad Karlshafen im Norden, von der Burgruine Merenberg im Westen bis zur Propstei Johannesberg im Osten erwarten Sie auf den kommenden Seiten kulturelle Schätze unseres Landes, beeindruckend in Szene gesetzt.

Unsere Liegenschaften sind nicht nur Zeugnisse hessischer, deutscher und europäischer Geschichte. Wir suchen sie auch auf, um uns zu bilden und zu erholen. Sie zeigen uns, wie Kunst und Handwerk sich über die Jahrhunderte entwickelt haben – und sie sind als beliebte Ausflugsziele auch ein unverzichtbarer wirtschaftlicher Faktor für die Regionen.

Wir freuen uns, wenn dieser Bildband Sie anregt, sich selbst ein Bild von unserem Engagement für diese Orte der Geschichte zu machen. Lassen Sie sich von Hessens Schätzen verzaubern!

Ihre
Angela Dorn
Hessische Ministerin
für Wissenschaft und Kunst

FOREWORD

Dear Reader,

This is a very special book, presenting all 48 castles, palaces, parks and individual monuments in the care of State Palaces and Gardens Hesse in one volume. From Fürstenlager State Park in the south to Bad Karlshafen Harbour Basin in the north, from Merenberg Castle Ruins in the west to the Johannesberg Provostry Buildings in the east, the cultural treasures of our region are revealed to impressive effect over the following pages.

Our sites are not merely witnesses to Hessian, German and European history. We also visit them to educate ourselves and to relax. They show us how arts and crafts have evolved over the centuries – and as popular attractions, they are also a vital economic factor for the region.

We hope that this book will inspire you to experience for yourself our commitment to these historic sites – and that you will be captivated by Hesse's treasures!

Regards.
Angela Dorn
*Hesse Minister
of Science and the Arts*

WILLKOMMEN

Liebe Leserinnen, liebe Leser,

natürlich ist es eine Binsenweisheit zu sagen, dass die Vergangenheit unser heutiges Leben beeinflusst. Sie ist auf Schritt und Tritt bei uns, fast nichts hat keine Geschichte. Die Vergangenheit führt uns vor Augen, woher wir kommen und wer wir sind. Denkmäler und andere Kulturgüter spielen dabei eine besondere Rolle. Sie erzählen als Gebäude, als Monumente, als Inventar von Schlössern, als Ausstellungsstücke, und auch als Gärten und Parks von dem, was früher einmal war.

Wer sich also mit vergangenen Zeiten beschäftigen will, ist bei uns an der richtigen oder vielmehr an den richtigen Adressen. Die Staatlichen Schlösser und Gärten Hessen betreuen eine Fülle unterschiedlichster Schlösser, Burgen, Klöster, Gärten und weitere Kleinodien. Sie reichen von Nord bis Süd und Ost bis West im Bundesland und umspannen 2000 Jahre Geschichte. Mit uns können Sie den Spuren der Römer am Limeswall und der Karolinger im Kloster Lorsch folgen, beide sind ebenso wie das Niederwalddenkmal, die Burgruine Ehrenfels und der Osteinsche Niederwald Welterbestätten der UNESCO. Sie können Orte erleben, die für die mittelalterlichen Staufer-Herrscher prägend waren, erkunden die Residenz eines Barockfürsten oder die privaten Appartements des letzten deutschen Kaiserpaares. Sie können großartige Stätten der Gartenkunst erleben, die im wahren Sinne des Wortes ‚gewachsen' sind.

Der Fotograf Michael Leukel kennt alle 48 Stätten des hessischen Kulturerbes in unserer Obhut, manche sogar wie seine Westentasche. Der vorliegende Band versammelt seine schönsten Ansichten und Einsichten, und es ist mir eine Freude, sie Ihnen vorzustellen. Diese Publikation fasst erstmals alle unsere Liegenschaften zwischen zwei Buchdeckeln zusammen. Mein großer Dank geht an Michael Leukel für dieses schöne Werk. Es ist gleichzeitig ein Aufruf, die vielfältigen Objekte und ihre Geschichten als Schätze anzusehen und sie für die Zukunft zu bewahren. Wir brauchen sie, wie sie uns brauchen. Nach gesetzlichem Auftrag und aus Leidenschaft setzen wir uns für ihren Erhalt ein.

Ihre
Kirsten Worms
Direktorin Staatliche Schlösser und Gärten Hessen

WELCOME

Dear Reader,

It goes without saying that the past influences our lives today. It is with us wherever we go, almost nothing has no history at all. The past reminds us of where we come from and who we are. Monuments and other cultural assets play a special role here. Buildings, monuments, palace inventories, exhibits and even gardens and parks tell us about how things used to be.

Anyone wishing to explore the past can therefore come to the right place (or places) with us. State Palaces and Gardens Hesse (Staatliche Schlösser und Gärten Hessen) curates an array of different palaces, castles, monasteries, gardens and other gems – ranging from north to south and east to west within the State of Hesse and spanning 2,000 years of history. Come with us to retrace the footsteps of the Romans on the Limes Wall or of the Carolingians at Lorsch Abbey, both of which are on the list of UNESCO World Heritage sites. Gain insights into places of importance during the medieval Staufen dynasty, into the residence of a Baroque

prince, or into the private apartments of the last German imperial couple. Or experience wonderful examples of truly flourishing garden design.

The photographer Michael Leukel is familiar with all 48 sites of Hessian cultural heritage in our care, and indeed knows some of them like the back of his hand. This book is a collection of his finest views and perspectives, and I am delighted to be able to present them to you in this way. This publication is the first time that all of our properties have been showcased together between the covers of a book. I should like to extend my gratitude to Michael Leukel for this beautiful work. It is at the same time an invitation to behold the many objects and their stories as treasures and to conserve them for the future. We need them in the same way that they need us. Both in accordance with our legal mandate and through our love for them, we are committed to their preservation.

Regards.
Kirsten Worms
Director, State Palaces and Gardens Hesse

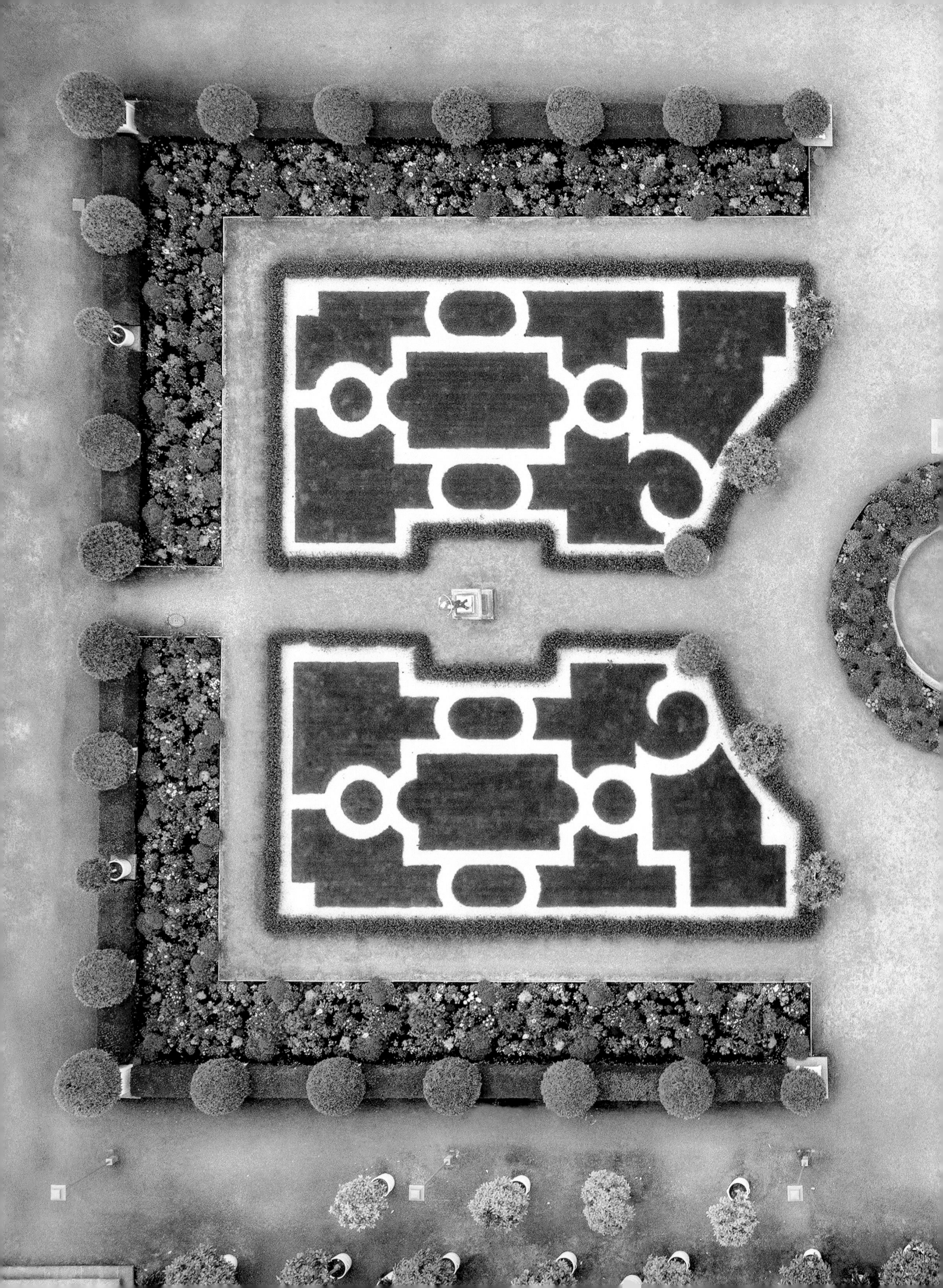

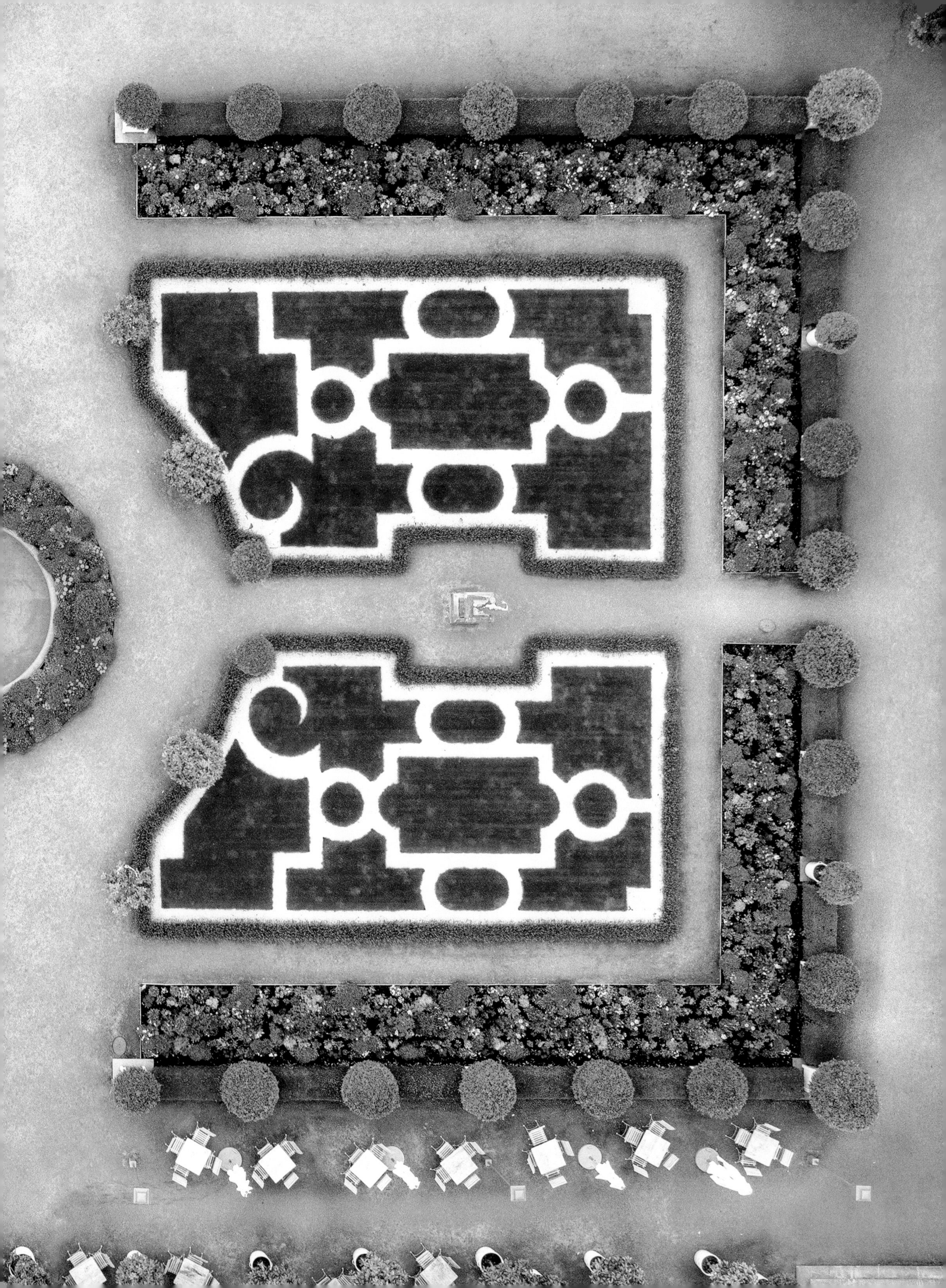

VORWORT UND DANK

Schlösser, Gärten, Burgen – historische Orte begeistern mich seit frühester Kindheit. Spannende und teils versteckte Ecken mit all ihren Details zu entdecken und diese in meiner Fotografie festzuhalten, sind meine große Leidenschaft. Mit diesen Aufnahmen den Menschen das Schöne in unserem unmittelbaren Umfeld zu zeigen, treibt mich auch zu nachtschlafenden Zeiten an diese Orte. So habe ich viele dieser Plätze kennen und lieben gelernt. Aufgrund der Nähe zu meinem Zuhause ist das Niederwalddenkmal ein Ort, den ich persönlich oft besuche. Majestätisch thront die Germania über dem Rhein bei Rüdesheim und erinnert dabei stets an die Schattenseiten des Krieges. Über eben dieses Denkmal und die ersten Fotografien, die ich dort in einer Schneenacht machte, entstand der Kontakt zu den Staatlichen Schlössern und Gärten Hessen im Jahr 2014. Hieraus entwickelten sich im Lauf der Zeit echte Freundschaften und nicht zuletzt auch der vorliegende Bildband.

Für die gute Zusammenarbeit, die dieses Buch erst ermöglicht hat, möchte ich an dieser Stelle Frau Kirsten Worms und Frau Dr. Katharina Bechler danken. Es steckt sehr viel Arbeit und Leidenschaft in solch einem Projekt.

Oft ist das Entscheiden für dieses oder jenes Foto nicht einfach, aber mit mehreren Augen findet man immer eine gute Lösung.

Ein Dankeschön geht auch an Frau Ursula Reinsch, die mein erster Kontakt nach Bad Homburg war und den Start mitgestaltet hat, und an Frau Elisabeth Weymann, die erheblich dazu beigetragen hat, meine Fotografien einem breiteren Publikum bekannt zu machen. Und selbstverständlich danke ich allen weiteren Mitarbeiter:innen der Staatlichen Schlösser und Gärten Hessen, die ich im Lauf der Jahre kennengelernt habe, und freue mich auf viele schöne Momente, die ich hoffentlich auch in Zukunft in den Liegenschaften in ganz Hessen verbringen werde.

Mein besonderer Dank gilt außerdem meiner Familie, die meine ganzen Fototouren duldsam mitmacht und mich in meiner Arbeit beständig unterstützt.

Und nun freue ich mich, die Leser:innen und Betrachter:innen mit auf meine Reise durch Hessens Kulturschätze zu nehmen, und wünsche viel Freude und spannende Entdeckungen in und mit diesem Buch!

Michael Leukel

FOREWORD AND ACKNOWLEDGEMENT

Palaces, gardens, castles – I have loved historical locations since my early childhood. Discovering fascinating and sometimes hidden corners with all their details and capturing them in my photographs is my passion. The opportunity to show people the beauty on our doorstep through my photos drives me to visit these localities even in the small hours of the night. This is how I have come to know and love many of these places.

The Niederwald Monument is close to my home and a place I often visit. Germania sits majestically above the River Rhine near Rüdesheim, a constant reminder of the darker sides of war. It was through this monument and the first photographs I took there on a wintry night that I first made contact with State Palaces and Gardens Hesse in 2014. This has led to genuine friendships and, most recently, to this photo book.

I should like to take this opportunity to thank Kirsten Worms and Dr. Katharina Bechler for the excellent cooperation during its production. Such a project involves a great deal of work and passion.

Deciding precisely which photo to use is not always easy, but several pairs of eyes always help to arrive at a good solution.

I should also like to thank Ursula Reinsch, my first contact in Bad Homburg, who helped shape the start of my journey. Additional thanks go to Elisabeth Weymann, who played a major role in making my photos known to a wider audience. And of course, I should like to thank all other employees of State Palaces and Gardens Hesse whom I have come to know over the years. I look forward to hopefully spending many more wonderful moments at the properties throughout Hesse in the future.

Finally, I extend special thanks to my family for patiently accompanying me on all my photo excursions and for constantly supporting me in my work.

I am delighted to be able to take you, as readers and viewers, along with me on my tour through Hesse's cultural treasures and hope you enjoy this book and the fascinating discoveries it holds in store.

Michael Leukel

48 KULTURSCHÄTZE AUF EINEN BLICK

1 Schloss und Schlosspark Bad Homburg, Bad Homburg vor der Höhe
2 Burgruine Oberreifenberg, Oberreifenberg
3 Burgruine Altweilnau, Weilrod-Altweilnau
4 Hutturm Walsdorf, Idstein-Walsdorf
5 Burgruine Hohenstein, Hohenstein
6 Burgruine Geroldstein, Heidenrod-Geroldstein
7 Schloss und Schlossgarten Weilburg, Weilburg
8 Burgruine Merenberg, Merenberg
9 Römerkastell Kleiner Feldberg, Glashütten
10 Römerkastell Kapersburg, Rosbach vor der Höhe
11 Römerbrunnen Kaichen, Kaichen
12 Fürstengruft Butzbach, Butzbach
13 Burgruine Münzenberg, Münzenberg
14 Adolfsturm und St. Georgsbrunnen, Burg Friedberg, Friedberg
15 Junker-Hansen-Turm, Neustadt
16 Elisabethbrunnen Schröck, Marburg-Schröck
17 Galgen von Hopfmannsfeld, Lautertal/Hopfmannsfeld
18 Hafenbecken Bad Karlshafen, Bad Karlshafen
19 Schloss Spangenberg, Spangenberg
20 Burgruine Felsberg, Felsberg
21 Burg Fürsteneck, Eiterfeld
22 Kloster Cornberg, Cornberg
23 Stiftsruine Bad Hersfeld, Bad Hersfeld
24 Propstei Johannesberg, Fulda
25 Kloster Konradsdorf, Ortenberg-Konradsdorf
26 Kaiserpfalz Gelnhausen, Gelnhausen
27 Kloster und Klostergarten Seligenstadt, Seligenstadt
28 Einhardsbasilika, Michelstadt-Steinbach
29 Kloster Lorsch, Lorsch, UNESCO-Welterbe
30 Staatspark Hanau-Wilhelmsbad, Hanau
31 Schloss Steinau, Steinau a. d. Straße
32 Burg- und Schlossruine Schwarzenfels, Sinntal-Schwarzenfels
33 Prinz-Georg-Garten, Darmstadt
34 Fürstengruft Darmstadt, Darmstadt
35 Burgruine Frankenstein, Mühltal
36 Staatspark Fürstenlager, Bensheim-Auerbach
37 Schloss Auerbach, Bensheim-Auerbach
38 Schlosspark Biebrich, Wiesbaden
39 Brentano-Haus, Oestrich-Winkel
40 Zeppelindenkmal, Trebur-Geinsheim
41 Burgruine Ehrenfels, Rüdesheim am Rhein
42 Osteinscher Niederwald, Rüdesheim am Rhein
43 Niederwalddenkmal, Rüdesheim am Rhein
44 Schloss Erbach, Erbach
45 Schloss Lichtenberg, Fischbachtal-Lichtenberg
46 Burg Breuberg, Breuberg
47 Veste Otzberg, Otzberg
48 Burg Hirschhorn, Hirschhorn

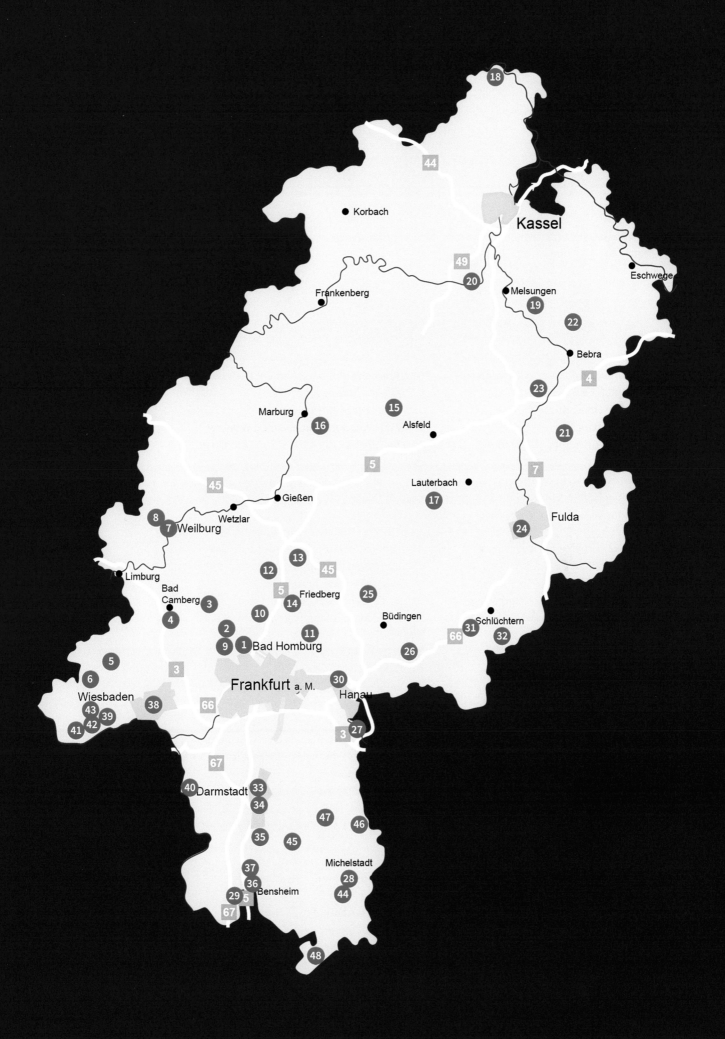

48 CULTURAL TREASURES AT A GLANCE

1   Bad Homburg Palace and Palace Park, Bad Homburg vor der Höhe
2   Oberreifenberg Castle Ruins, Oberreifenberg
3   Altweilnau Castle Ruins, Weilrod-Altweilnau
4   Hutturm Tower Walsdorf, Idstein-Walsdorf
5   Hohenstein Castle Ruins, Hohenstein
6   Geroldstein Castle Ruins, Heidenrod-Geroldstein
7   Weilburg Palace and Palace Gardens, Weilburg
8   Merenberg Castle Ruins, Merenberg
9   Roman Fort of Kleiner Feldberg, Glashütten
10 Roman Fort of Kapersburg, Rosbach vor der Höhe
11 Roman Well Kaichen, Kaichen
12 The Fürstengruft Princely Crypt Butzbach, Butzbach
13 Münzenberg Castle Ruins, Münzenberg
14 Adolf's Tower and the St George Fountain, Friedberg Castle, Friedberg
15 Junker-Hansen Tower, Neustadt
16 The Elisabeth Fountain, Schröck, Marburg-Schröck
17 The Gallows of Hopfmannsfeld, Lautertal/Hopfmannsfeld
18 Bad Karlshafen Harbour Basin, Bad Karlshafen
19 Spangenberg Palace, Spangenberg
20 Felsberg Castle Ruins, Felsberg
21 Fürsteneck Castle, Eiterfeld
22 Cornberg Monastery, Cornberg
23 Bad Hersfeld Collegiate Church Ruins, Bad Hersfeld
24 Johannesberg Provostry Buildings, Fulda
25 Konradsdorf Monastery, Ortenberg-Konradsdorf
26 Imperial Palace of Gelnhausen, Gelnhausen
27 Seligenstadt Abbey and Abbey Garden, Seligenstadt
28 Einhard's Basilica, Michelstadt-Steinbach
29 Lorsch Abbey, Lorsch, UNESCO World Heritage Site
30 Hanau-Wilhelmsbad State Park, Hanau
31 Steinau Palace, Steinau an der Straße
32 Schwarzenfels Castle and Palace Ruins, Sinntal-Schwarzenfels
33 Prince George Garden, Darmstadt
34 The Fürstengruft Princely Crypt Darmstadt, Darmstadt
35 Frankenstein Castle Ruins, Mühltal
36 Fürstenlager State Park, Bensheim-Auerbach
37 Auerbach Palace, Bensheim-Auerbach
38 Biebrich Palace Park, Wiesbaden
39 Brentano House, Oestrich-Winkel
40 Zeppelin Monument, Trebur-Geinsheim
41 Ehrenfels Castle Ruins, Rüdesheim am Rhein
42 Ostein's Niederwald Park, Rüdesheim am Rhein
43 Niederwald Monument, Rüdesheim am Rhein
44 Erbach Palace, Erbach
45 Lichtenberg Palace, Fischbachtal-Lichtenberg
46 Breuberg Castle, Breuberg
47 Otzberg Fortress, Otzberg
48 Hirschhorn Castle, Hirschhorn

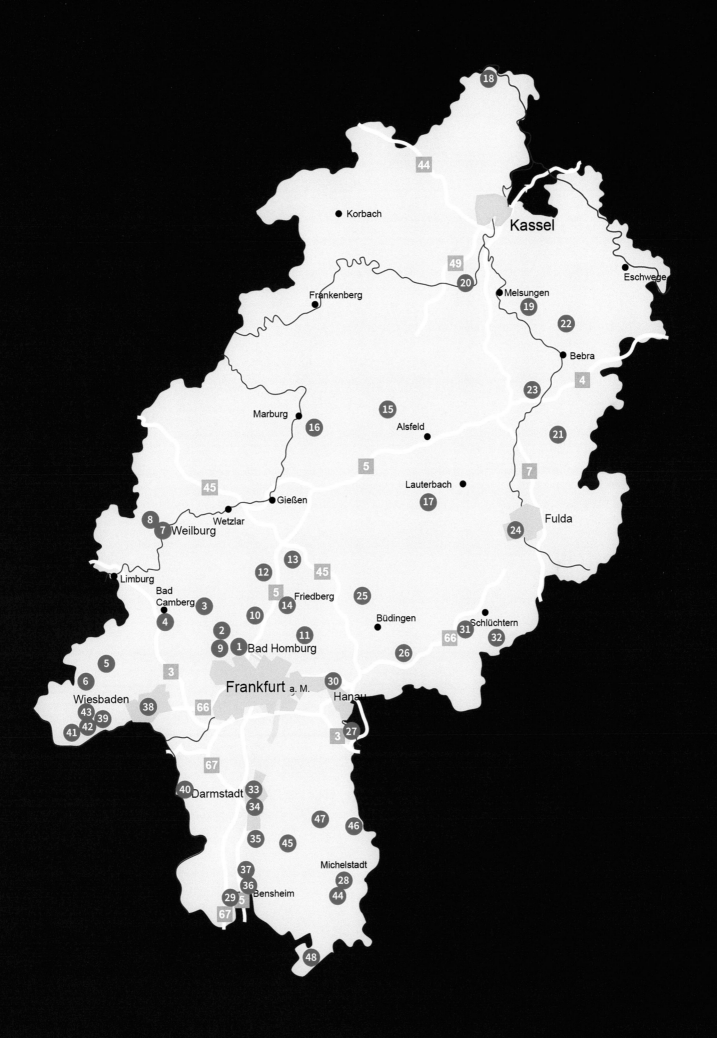

IM TAUNUS

IN THE TAUNUS REGION

SCHLOSS UND SCHLOSSPARK BAD HOMBURG

BAD HOMBURG PALACE AND PALACE PARK

Schloss Bad Homburg, einst Residenz der Landgrafen von Hessen-Homburg sowie später die Sommerresidenz der drei letzten deutschen Kaiser, ist heute Hauptsitz der Staatlichen Schlösser und Gärten Hessen. Noch immer wacht der Bergfried der mittelalterlichen Burg, der Weiße Turm, über der barocken Schlossanlage und ist heute prominentes Wahrzeichen der Kurstadt.

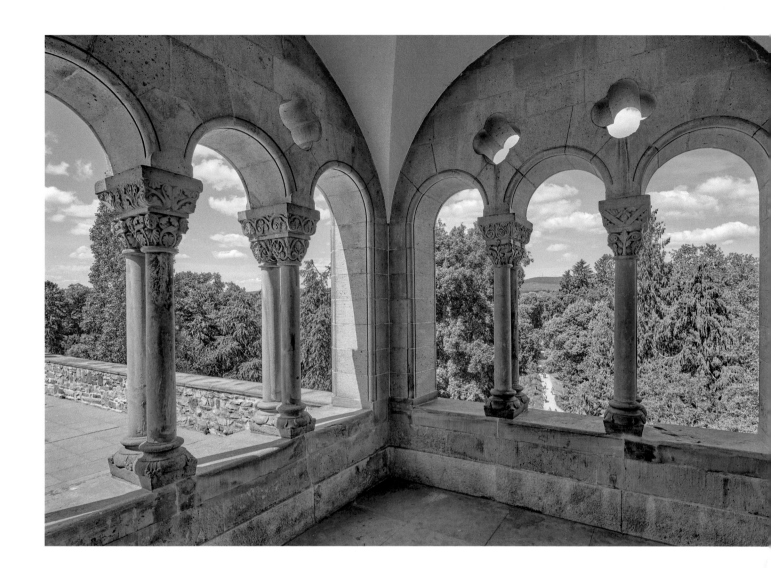

▲ Arkaden der Romanischen Halle
Arcades of the Romanesque Hall

◄ Oberer Schlosshof mit dem
Weißen Turm
*Upper palace courtyard with
the White Tower*

Schloss Bad Homburg verdankt sein heutiges Erscheinungsbild Landgraf Friedrich II. (1633–1708), der die mittelalterliche Burg 1680 abreißen und an ihrer Stelle ein schlichtes frühbarockes Schloss errichten ließ. Weitere Umbauten folgten im 19. und frühen 20. Jahrhundert.

Der Schlosspark, der ebenfalls durch Friedrich II. in barocken Strukturen und mit Orangerie angelegt wurde, erfuhr durch das Landgrafenpaar Friedrich V. (1748–1820) und Karoline (1746–1821) sowie deren als britische Königstocher geborene Schwiegertochter Elizabeth (1770–1840) eine naturnahe Umgestaltung im englischen Landschaftsstil. Dabei wurde der Schloss-

park über seine Grenzen hinaus durch die Anlage der Landgräflichen Gartenlandschaft erweitert: Entlang einer nach Nordwesten verlaufenden Achse reihten sich Gärten und gestaltete Waldpartien über mehrere Kilometer schnurgerade auf – ein Gesamtkunstwerk, das heute in Teilen erhalten ist.

Im Schloss ist die Witwenwohnung von Elizabeth von Interesse und vor allem die Appartements, die der letzte deutsche Kaiser Wilhelm II. (1859–1941) und seine Frau Auguste Victoria (1858–1921) bei ihren Aufenthalten in der international renommierten Kurstadt Bad Homburg bewohnten. Letztere geben einen einzigartigen Einblick in kaiserzeitliche Wohnkultur.

▲ Arbeitszimmer der Kaiserin
Auguste Victoria
*Study of the Empress Auguste
Victoria*

▶ Pendule mit Darstellung des
Herkules (Detail)
*Clock with depiction of Hercules
(close-up view)*

▶▶ Haupttreppe im Königsflügel
Main staircase in the King's Wing

Bad Homburg Palace, once the residence of the landgraves of Hesse-Homburg and subsequently the summer residence of the last three German Emperors, is today the administrative headquarters of State Palaces and Gardens Hesse (Staatliche Schlösser und Gärten Hessen). The keep of the medieval castle, known as the White Tower, still stands guard over the Baroque palace complex and is the spa town's most prominent landmark.

▶ Speisesaal im Englischen Flügel
Dining room in the English Wing

▼ Zedern vor dem Königsflügel
Cedars in front of the King's Wing

Bad Homburg Palace owes its current appearance to Landgrave Friedrich II (1633–1708), who demolished the medieval castle in 1680 and replaced it with a sombre Early Baroque palace. Further modifications took place in the 19th and early 20th centuries.

Landgrave Friedrich V (1748–1820) and his wife Landgravine Caroline (1746–1821), as well as their daughter-in-law Elizabeth (1770–1840) who was a British princess by birth, restyled the palace park, which had also been designed with Baroque structures and an organgery by Friedrich II, into a natural space based on the fashion for English gardens. The palace park was expanded beyond its boundaries through the creation of the landgraviate garden landscape, with gardens and structured woodland areas extending in a straight line for several kilometres along an axis running to the north-west. Parts of this coalescence of design have been recreated today.

Particular highlights in the palace include Elizabeth's widow's apartment, and also the apartments which the last German emperor, William II (1859–1941), and his wife Auguste Victoria (1858–1921) occupied during their visits to the internationally renowned spa town of Bad Homburg. These apartments offer a unique insight into interior decoration during imperial times.

Schloss und Schlosspark
Bad Homburg
61348 Bad Homburg
vor der Höhe
www.schloesser-hessen.de/
de/schloss-bad-homburg

BURGRUINE OBERREIFENBERG

OBERREIFENBERG CASTLE RUINS

Die Ruine Reifenberg ist die höchstgelegene mittelalterliche Burg im Taunus. Dank ihrer Lage auf einem Felssporn über Oberreifenberg bietet sie bis heute einen imposanten Anblick. In ihren Glanzzeiten soll sich der Stammsitz der Reiffenberger über eine ummauerte Fläche von 25 000 Quadratmetern erstreckt haben. Bis zur Schleifung Ende des 17. Jahrhunderts war die Burg bewohnbar.

Burgruine Oberreifenberg
Schlossstraße
61389 Oberreifenberg
www.schloesser-hessen.de/
de/burgruine-oberreifenberg

Der Baubeginn der Burg Reifenberg ist nicht bekannt, erst 1234 wird sie indirekt in einer Urkunde erwähnt. Sie war Stammsitz des Geschlechts der Reiffenberger, die in zahlreiche Fehden verwickelt waren. Daher erlebte die Burg auch mehrfache Zerstörungen, sie wurde jedoch bis zu ihrer endgültigen Schleifung im Jahr 1689 immer wieder aufgebaut. Ursprünglich bestand sie aus einer dreiteiligen, stark gesicherten Innen- und einer Vorburg, deren Ringmauer den nördlichen Zwinger einschloss.

Sichtbar sind heute noch Teile der Wehranlage und die Ruinen militärischer, ziviler und sakraler Bauten aus unterschiedlichen Entwicklungsphasen der Anlage. Neben dem Bergfried sind dies unter anderem eine mächtige, vier Meter dicke Schildmauer mit Rundtürmen, ein Kirchenkeller und ein sehr schlanker, hoher Wohnturm: Dieser reichte einst über sechs Stockwerke. Ganz oben befindet sich heute eine Plattform, die über eine steinerne Wendeltreppe erreichbar ist und eine herrliche Aussicht über das obere Weiltal zum Großen Feldberg bietet.

The Reifenberg ruins are the remains of the highest medieval castle in the Taunus mountain range. Sitting on a rocky promontory above Oberreifenberg, they are still an imposing sight today. In its heyday, the ancestral seat of the Reiffenbergs is said to have extended over a walled area of 25,000 square metres. The castle was habitable until its demolition at the end of the 17th century.

It is not known when construction began on Reifenberg castle, which is first mentioned only indirectly in a document dating back to 1234. It was the ancestral seat of the house of Reiffenberg, which was involved in numerous feuds. As a result, the castle was destroyed on several occasions, but was repeatedly rebuilt until its final demolition in 1689. Originally, it consisted of a heavily fortified three-part inner castle and an outer bailey, whose curtain wall enclosed the northern ward.

Parts of the defensive system and the ruins of military, civil and religious structures from the complex's various phases of development are still visible today. As well as the keep, these include a massive, four-metre-thick defensive wall with round towers, a church cellar, and a tall, very slender residential tower. This once extended over six storeys. The very top of the tower now houses a platform, accessible via a stone spiral staircase and offering wonderful views over the upper Weiltal Valley towards Großer Feldberg.

BURGRUINE ALTWEILNAU

ALTWEILNAU CASTLE RUINS

Über den Fachwerkhäusern von Altweilnau, das heute zu Weilrod im Taunus gehört, ragt der Bergfried der Burgruine empor. Wer hinaufsteigt, wird mit einem wunderschönen Panoramablick über den Ort und die hügelige Landschaft des Weiltals belohnt.

The keep of the castle ruins rises above the half-timbered houses of Altweilnau, which today forms part of Weilrod in the Taunus region. Visitors braving the climb are rewarded with a wonderful panoramic view of the locality and the hilly landscape of the Weiltal Valley.

Burg Altweilnau wurde im Jahr 1208 erstmals urkundlich erwähnt und wahrscheinlich kurz zuvor anstelle eines Vorgängerbaus hoch über dem Weiltal errichtet. Dendochronologische Untersuchungen an der hölzernen Bausubstanz des gut erhaltenen Bergfrieds ergaben, dass dessen Erbauung ziemlich genau auf 1203/04 zu datieren ist. Die Grafen von Diez ließen die Festungsanlage errichten. Dank ihrer Lage hoch über dem Tal diente sie lange Zeit als Beobachtungsposten und Wohnburg. Die Anlage umgab eine wehrhafte Ringmauer. Bezeugt sind außerdem weitere Gebäude, wie das gräfliche Wohnhaus, Ställe und Scheunen, die aber nicht erhalten sind. In den folgenden Jahrhunderten erlebte die Burg mehrere Besitzerwechsel. So gehörte sie unter anderem den Herren von Eppstein und ab dem 16. Jahrhundert den Grafen von Nassau-Weilburg. Spätestens ab 1608 war die Burg nicht mehr bewohnbar.

Heute ist der Bergfried frei zugänglich. Der runde, knapp 18 Meter hohe Bergfried am höchsten Punkt der Anlage ist mit einer Aussichtsplattform versehen. Außerdem haben sich der Halsgraben an der Nordostseite sowie Teile der geräumigen Ringmauer mit dem Rest eines Schalenturmes erhalten.

Altweilnau Castle was first mentioned in documents in 1208 and was probably constructed just before then to replace a previous building high above the Weiltal Valley. Dendochronological studies of the wooden structure of the well-preserved keep revealed that this building can be fairly accurately dated to 1203/04.

The fortification was commissioned by the counts of Diez. Situated high above the valley, it served as a lookout post and residential castle for a long time. The complex was surrounded by a mighty curtain wall. Although evidence of other buildings (such as the Counts' residence, stables and barns) exists, they have not been pre-served. The castle saw several changes of ownership over the ensuing centuries. Among others, it belonged to the Lords of Eppstein and, from the 16th century, to the Counts of Nassau-Weilburg. The castle had become uninhabitable by 1608 at the latest.

The keep is freely accessible today. The round keep, almost 18 metres high, is situated at the highest point of the castle complex and has a viewing platform. The neck ditch on the north-eastern side and parts of the extensive curtain wall with the remains of a shell tower have also been preserved.

Burgruine Altweilnau
61276 Weilrod-Altweilnau
www.schloesser-hessen.de/
de/burgruine-altweilnau

HUTTURM WALSDORF
HUTTURM TOWER WALSDORF

Der Hutturm in Walsdorf, das heute zu Idstein im Taunus gehört, ist das Wahrzeichen des Ortes und ein wunderbarer Aussichtspunkt. Er wurde im späten 14. Jahrhundert als Teil der neuen Stadtmauer errichtet. Damals erhob Graf Adolf I. von Nassau-Idstein (um 1307–1370), dessen Herrschaft Walsdorf seit 1355 unterstand, den Ort zum Freiflecken, womit er stadtähnliche Rechte erhielt.

Hutturm Walsdorf
Hainstraße 13
65510 Idstein-Walsdorf
www.schloesser-hessen.de/
de/hutturm-walsdorf

Bereits 774 wurde Walsdorf im Lorscher Codex erstmals erwähnt. Zusammen mit der Erhebung zum Freiflecken erfolgte im 14. Jahrhundert unter den Grafen von Nassau-Idstein die Verlegung des Ortes vom Tal auf eine langgestreckte Anhöhe oberhalb des Emsbachs. Damals umgab man Walsdorf zudem mit einer Stadtmauer, die zwei Stadttore sowie mehrere Türme hatte. Der runde Hutturm ist bis heute als höchster unter ihnen erhalten.

Er hat einen Durchmesser von rund 7,50 Meter und ist 24 Meter hoch, die Bruchsteinmauern sind bis zu 1,80 Meter dick. Sein Inneres ist heute wieder begehbar und mit einer Aussichtsplattform versehen, die wunderbare Ausblicke in die umgebende Landschaft gewährt. Der Name des Turms hat übrigens nichts mit der gleichnamigen Kopfbedeckung zu tun, sondern kommt wahrscheinlich daher, dass der Bau einst als Wachturm die Bevölkerung ,behütete'. Außerdem stellte der Graf zu Nassau-Idstein die Wachen – das Bauwerk stand also unter gräflicher ,Obhut'.

The Hutturm Tower in Walsdorf, which today belongs to Idstein in the Taunus region, serves as a landmark for the locality and offers a magnificent vantage point. It was built in the late 14th century as part of the new town wall. At the time, Count Adolf I of Nassau-Idstein (around 1307–1370), who had governed Walsdorf since 1355, elevated the locality to a "Freiflecken", meaning it received rights similar to that of a town.

Walsdorf was first mentioned as early as 774 in the Lorsch Codex. In the 14th century and in conjunction with its elevation to a Freiflecken, the locality was relocated, under the Counts of Nassau-Idstein, from the valley to an elongated hill above the Emsbach River. Walsdorf was then also encircled by a town wall containing two town gates and several towers. The round Hutturm is the tallest of these towers and is still preserved today.

It has a diameter of around 7.50 metres and is 24 metres high. The quarry-stone walls are up to 1.80 metres thick. It is now possible to visit the inside of the keep and ascend to a viewing platform offering magnificent views over the surrounding landscape. The name of the tower actually has nothing to do with the German word for hat ("Hut") and is more probably connected to the German verb "behüten" and the fact that the structure once served as a watchtower to "protect" the population. The Count of Nassau-Idstein also provided the guards – meaning the structure was under the custody ("Obhut") of the Count.

BURGRUINE HOHENSTEIN

HOHENSTEIN CASTLE RUINS

Die Burgruine Hohenstein thront prominent über dem waldreichen Aartal nicht weit von Bad Schwalbach. Die einst prachtvolle, eng bebaute Burganlage wurde im Dreißigjährigen Krieg (1618–1648) zur Ruine – und ist bis heute eines der größten und beeindruckendsten Kulturdenkmale des Taunus.

The Hohenstein Castle Ruins sit majestically above the wooded Aartal Valley not far from Bad Schwalbach. The once imposing, tightly arranged castle complex fell into ruin during the Thirty Years' War (1618–1648) and today remains one of the largest and most impressive cultural monuments in the Taunus mountain range.

Eine Nebenlinie der Grafen von Katzenelnbogen erbaute sich um 1190 die „Hoynstein" – als Bollwerk im Grenzgebiet zu den Territorien der Erzbistümer Mainz und Trier sowie der Grafschaft Nassau-Idstein. Der Stammsitz der Grafenfamilie, die Burg Katzenelnbogen, lag nur 15 Kilometer entfernt. Im frühen 15. Jahrhundert erfolgte ein erster größerer Ausbau der Anlage.
Mit dem Aussterben der Katzenelnbogener 1479 fiel die Burg an Hessen. Landgraf Moritz von Hessen-Kassel (1572–1632) war es, der die Anlage um 1600 aufwendig umbaute und modernisierte. Kolorierte Grundrisse und Aufrisse seines Baumeisters Wilhelm Dilich (1571–1650) zeugen von ihrer einstigen Pracht: Sie zeigen die Kernburg auf Spornesspitze, darunter die winkelförmige Vorburg, Halsgraben und Zugbrücke, alles eng bebaut. Es verwundert nicht, dass der Landgraf gerne auf Burg Hohenstein residierte. Doch die Blütezeit währte nur kurz: 1647 geriet die Burg unter Beschuss und verfiel seitdem. Was blieb, ist überaus sehenswert: Neben der Lage beeindrucken vor allem der sechseckige Bergfried und die von hohen sechsgeschossigen Türmen eingefasste innere Schildmauer mit Schlitzscharten und Wehrgang.

Burgruine Hohenstein
Burgstraße 12
65329 Hohenstein
www.schloesser-hessen.de/
de/burgruine-hohenstein

A collateral line of the Counts of Katzenelnbogen built the "Hoynstein" around 1190 as a stronghold in the area bordering the territories of the Archbishoprics of Mainz and Trier and the County of Nassau-Idstein. The ancestral seat of the Counts' family, Katzenelnbogen Castle, was only 15 kilometres away. The castle underwent its first major extension in the early 15th century.

The castle fell to Hesse in 1479 when the Katzenelnbogen line died out. Landgrave Moritz of Hesse-Kassel (1572–1632) subsequently carried out extensive remodelling and modernisation work at the castle around 1600. Coloured floor plans and elevations by his builder Wilhelm Dilich (1571–1650) testify to the castle's former splendour. They show the central part of the castle on the top of the spur, and below it the angled bailey, neck ditch and drawbridge, all built closely together. It is hardly surprising that the landgrave enjoyed residing at Hohenstein Castle.

However, its heyday was short-lived. In 1647 the castle came under attack and subsequently fell into decay. The remains are well worth seeing: besides the location, visitors will in particular also be impressed by the hexagonal keep and by the inner defensive wall with its tall, six-storey towers and slit embrasures and battlements.

BURGRUINE GEROLDSTEIN

GEROLDSTEIN CASTLE RUINS

Die Burgruine Geroldstein aus dem späten 12. Jahrhundert sitzt auf einem steil abfallenden Felsvorsprung über dem gleichnamigen Taunusörtchen. Vom Aufstieg derer von Geroldstein zeugt, dass die Familie sich im 14. Jahrhundert einen Steinwurf entfernt mit Burg Haneck eine zweite, deutlich größere Anlage errichten ließ. So schmückt sich Geroldstein, Ortsteil von Heidenrod, heute mit zwei romantischen Burgruinen.

Burg Geroldstein liegt heute am Süd-ufer der Wisper. Einst zog der Fluss eine Schleife um den Felssporn. Zusammen mit dem steil abfallenden Gelände war die Spornburg somit von drei Seiten gut geschützt. Von der vierten, zum Berg gewandten Seite, wurden die für ihren Bau benötigten Steine gebrochen, sodass zwischen Berg und Burg ein tiefer Halsgraben entstand.

1215 fand die Burg als „Gerardstein" erstmals urkundliche Erwähnung. Lehensherren der Geroldsteiner waren die Grafen von Katzenelnbogen. Die Burg, die an einem wichtigen Verbindungsweg zum Rhein lag, trug zum Schutz der Grenzen zwischen deren Einflussgebiet und dem Territorium des Erzstiftes Mainz bei. Die Burg verfiel nach Aussterben des hier lebenden Rittergeschlechtes am Ende des 16. Jahrhunderts zur Ruine.

Leider lassen die Reste des Bruchsteinmauerwerks keinen eindeutigen Schluss auf die genaue Grundform und Ausdehnung der Anlage zu. In der etwa zweieinhalb Meter dicken Schildmauer öffnet sich ein kleines Tor, das in den einstigen Burghof führt. Außerdem sind ein in die Ringmauer integrierter siebeneckiger Bergfried sowie das Fundament eines weiteren Turmes erhalten.

The Geroldstein Castle Ruins date back to the late 12th century and sit on a precipitous promontory overlooking the village of the same name in the Taunus mountain range. The rise of the Geroldstein family is evidenced by the fact that in the 14th century it built a second, considerably larger complex, Haneck Castle, just a stone's throw away. As a result, the village of Geroldstein, a district of Heidenrod, is now graced by two Romantic castle ruins.

Burgruine Geroldstein
65321 Heidenrod-Geroldstein
www.schloesser-hessen.de/de/burgruine-geroldstein

Geroldstein Castle now lies on the south bank of the Wisper River. The river once looped around the castle rock, ensuring that combined with the steep terrain, the spur castle was well protected from three sides. The stones required for the castle's construction were taken from the fourth side facing the mountain, thus creating a deep neck ditch between the castle and the mountain.

The castle was first mentioned as "Gerardstein" in records dating back to 1215. The feudal lords of the Geroldsteins were the Counts of Katzenelnbogen. The castle, which was located on an important connecting route to the River Rhine, played a contributory role in protecting the borders between the Counts' zone of influence and the territory of the Archbishopric of Mainz. After the knightly family that lived here died out at the end of the 16th century, the castle fell to ruin.

Unfortunately, the remains of the quarry stone walls do not allow any clear conclusion about the complex's precise basic format or its extent. The defensive wall, which is around two and a half metres thick, has an opening for a small gatehouse that leads to the castle's former courtyard. A heptagonal keep integrated into the curtain wall and the foundations of a further tower have also been preserved.

WEILBURG UND UMGEBUNG

WEILBURG AND THE SURROUNDING AREA

SCHLOSS UND SCHLOSSGARTEN WEILBURG

WEILBURG PALACE AND PALACE GARDENS

Schloss und Schlossgarten Weilburg erzählen vom höfischen Lebensgefühl zu Beginn des 18. Jahrhunderts. Damals ließ Graf Johann Ernst zu Nassau-Weilburg (1664–1719) in seiner Residenzstadt eine Vision Wirklichkeit werden. Vorbild war ihm das Versailles des Sonnenkönigs Ludwig XIV. (1638–1715). Kein Wunder also, dass Weilburg später den Beinamen „Perle an der Lahn" erhielt.

Schloss und
Schlossgarten Weilburg
Schloßplatz
35781 Weilburg
www.schloesser-hessen.de/
de/schloss-weilburg

▲ Die Obere Orangerie
The Upper Orangery

◄ Vergoldete Bleiskulptur eines
antiken Cymbalspielers vor der
Unteren Orangerie
*Gilded lead sculpture of an ancient
cymbal player in front of the Lower
Orangery*

Ab 1702 ließ Graf Johann Ernst zu Nassau-Weilburg die bestehende vierflügelige Renaissanceanlage in Weilburg
sowie die noch mittelalterlich geprägte
Stadt durch seinen Baumeister Julius
Ludwig Rothweil (1676–1750) zu einer
barocken Residenz um- und ausbauen.
Im Mittelpunkt der Bautätigkeit stand
das auf einem hohen Bergsporn gelegene Schloss. Auch die Innenausstattung
wurde den Ansprüchen barocker
Prachtentfaltung angepasst. Bis heute
hat sich die gräfliche Badewanne aus
schwarzem Marmor erhalten. Weitere
Höhepunkte sind das Kürfürstliche
Gemach und das sogenannte Chinakabinett.

Auch den Weilburger Schlossgarten ließ
Johann Ernst nach barocken Prinzipien neu gestalten und als Ort eleganter Amüsements für die Hofgesellschaft herrichten. Aufgrund der Lage
am Hang teilt sich der nach Süden ausgerichtete Garten in mehrere Parterres
mit gleich zwei Orangerien zur Überwinterung der Zitruspflanzen. Ein Spaziergang durch das Lindenboskett im
oberen Parterre führt zu der mit großen
grün-goldenen Vasen geschmückten
Balustrade und weiter zum unteren
Parterre, wo es sich herrlich über die
weißen Wege flanieren und bei Statuen,
Brunnen und Sonnenuhr verweilen
lässt.

Weilburg Palace and Palace Gardens chronicle courtly life at the beginning of the 18th century. This was when Count Johann Ernst of Nassau-Weilburg (1664–1719) realised his vision to model his residence town on Versailles, the palace of King Louis XIV, the Sun King (1638–1715). It is hardly surprising, therefore, that Weilburg later become known as the "Pearl on the Lahn".

▲ Das Untere Parterre mit der Unteren Orangerie
The Lower Parterre with the lower orangery

◄ Hölzerner Gang
Wooden hallway

◄ Möbeldetail im Schlafgemach der Fürstin Louise Isabelle von Nassau-Weilburg
Close-up of furniture in the bed chamber of Princess Louise Isabelle of Nassau-Weilburg

▲ Das Kurfürstliche Gemach
The Electoral Chamber

From 1702, Count Johann Ernst of Nassau-Weilburg commissioned his builder Julius Ludwig Rothweil (1676–1750) to modify and expand the existing four-winged Renaissance complex in Weilburg and its surrounding town, which still bore a medieval stamp, to create a Baroque residence. The construction works centred on the palace, which sits on a high mountain spur. The interior was also designed to meet the demands of Baroque splendour. The Count's huge black marble bathtub has been preserved to this day. Other highlights include the Elector's Chamber and what is known as the Chinese Room.

Johann Ernst also had Weilburg's palace gardens redesigned according to Baroque aesthetics, creating a place of elegant amusement for court society. With its hillside location, the south-facing garden is divided into several parterres and includes two orangeries for overwintering citrus plants. A walk through the grove of lime trees in the upper garden leads to a balustrade adorned with large green-gold vases and onward to the Lower Parterre, where visitors can stroll along the white paths and linger among statues, fountains and a sundial.

BURGRUINE MERENBERG

MERENBERG CASTLE RUINS

Das Großherzogtum Luxemburg und die mittelhessische Ortschaft Merenberg trennen 250 Kilometer. Auf den ersten Blick haben sie nichts gemein. Und doch trägt der heutige Großherzog von Luxemburg den Titel eines Herrn von Merenberg. Durch geschickte Heiratspolitik verband sich die Familie mit den großen Adelshäusern Europas. Die Ruine ihrer Stammburg erhebt sich noch heute hoch über dem Lahntal.

Burgruine Merenberg
Schloßbergweg
35799 Merenberg
www.schloesser-hessen.de/
de/burgruine-merenberg

Als Tor zum Westerwald lag Burg Merenberg an der alten Handelsstraße Frankfurt-Siegen-Köln. Die Burgherren boten den Reisenden Schutz, erhoben Wegezoll und legten den Grundstein für den eigenen gesellschaftlichen Aufstieg.

Ab dem 12. Jahrhundert ist die Familie der Merenberger in der Region nachweisbar, wo sie über ausgedehnte Ländereien verfügte. Letzter Vertreter des Geschlechts war Hartrad VI. (1288–1328), der zwei Töchter, jedoch keinen männlichen Erben hatte. Dank eines vom König verliehenen Privilegs ging der Besitz nach seinem Tod an die Tochter Gertrud über, welche 1333 Johann I. von Nassau-Weilburg (1309–1371) heiratete. Die Nassau-Weilburger wurden im 19. Jahrhundert durch Erbfolge Großherzöge von Luxemburg. So hat sich der Name der Merenberger bis heute erhalten; doch ihr Stammsitz, die Burg Merenberg, brannte im Dreißigjährigen Krieg (1618–1648) ab und blieb seitdem Ruine.

Von der langgezogenen, rechteckigen Anlage zeugen heute Reste der Außenmauern und des einst dreistöckigen Palas sowie der 22 Meter hohe, runde Bergfried. Letzterer dient als Aussichtsturm und bietet einen herrlichen Rundblick in die Natur des Lahntals bis hin zum Feldberg.

Separated by 250 kilometres, at first glance the Grand Duchy of Luxembourg and the town of Merenberg in central Hesse would appear to have nothing in common. And yet the current Grand Duke of Luxembourg bears the title of a lord of Merenberg. A skilful marriage policy ensured that the family acquired connections with Europe's great noble houses. The ruins of their ancestral castle still rise high above the Lahn Valley today.

As the gateway to the Westerwald region, Merenberg Castle lay on the old trade road linking Frankfurt, Siegen and Cologne. The lords of the castle offered protection to travellers, collected tolls, and laid the foundations for their own social advancement.

Evidence of the Merenberg family in the region exists from the 12th century when they owned extensive estates. The last representative of the house was Hartrad VI (1288–1328), who had two daughters but no male heirs. Following a privilege granted by the king, ownership passed to Hartrad's daughter Gertrud on his death. She married Johann I of Nassau Weilburg (1309–1371) in 1333. In the 19th century, the Nassau Weilburgs became Grand Dukes of Luxembourg through succession. The Merenberg name has thus been preserved to this day, although the family's ancestral seat, Merenberg Castle, burnt down in the Thirty Years' War (1618–1648) and has remained in ruins ever since.

Remains of the outer walls and of the great hall, formerly consisting of three floors, and of the 22-metre-high round keep bear witness to the elongated rectangular castle complex. The keep serves as a lookout tower and offers a spectacular panoramic view over the natural landscape of the Lahn Valley to Feldberg.

UNESCO-WELTERBE GRENZEN DES RÖMISCHEN REICHES IM TAUNUS

UNESCO WORLD HERITAGE SITE "FRONTIERS OF THE ROMAN EMPIRE" IN THE TAUNUS REGION

RÖMERKASTELL KLEINER FELDBERG, GLASHÜTTEN

ROMAN FORT OF KLEINER FELDBERG, GLASHÜTTEN

Das Feldbergkastell im Taunus war einst Teil der Außengrenzen des Römischen Reiches. Heute gehört es zur UNESCO-Welterbestätte „Grenzen des Römischen Reiches", die den Hadrians- und Antoninuswall in Großbritannien und den Obergermanisch-Raetischen Limes umfasst. Von römischen Wehrmauern und Gräben, Kastellen und Holztürmen zeugen heute vor allem Überreste im Boden.

Das gut restaurierte Kastell Kleiner Feldberg liegt inmitten von hohen Bäumen zwischen Kleinem und Großem Feldberg im Taunus und gehört damit zum besterhaltenen Abschnitt des Limes. Es entstand nach der Mitte des 2. Jahrhunderts, als der Druck der Germanen auf die Grenzen des Imperiums zunahm.

In der Garnison war eine teilberittene Erkundungseinheit von 150 bis 200 Mann stationiert. Das Kastell erhob sich über einem rechteckigen Grundriss mit einer Fläche von 78 x 93 Metern. Es war von einem Graben umgeben, besaß Ecktürme, vier Tore und die typischen Innenbauten römischer Lager. Heute präsentiert sich die Stätte als archäologische Parklandschaft. Erhalten ist die Umwehrung des Kastells, die Apsis des Fahnenheiligtums und Mauerzüge des Kommandantenhauses und des Speichergebäudes. Außerdem haben sich Reste eines vorgelagerten „balnearium" mit Kalt- und Heißbad erhalten. Viele Funde der Feldberggarnison befinden sich heute im rekonstruierten Kastell Saalburg bei Bad Homburg vor der Höhe.

The Fort at Feldberg in the Taunus mountain range was once part of the outer frontiers of the Roman Empire. It is today part of UNESCO's World Heritage site "Frontiers of the Roman Empire", which includes Hadrian's Wall and the Antonine Wall in Great Britain as well as the Upper German-Raetian Limes. Today, it is mainly remains in the ground that bear testimony to Roman defensive walls and ditches, forts and wooden towers.

The well-restored fort of Kleiner Feldberg is situated in a forest between Kleiner and Großer Feldberg in the Taunus region and is part of the Limes' best-preserved section. It was built after the middle of the second century, when the Germans increased their pressure on the borders of the Roman Empire.

The garrison housed a partially mounted unit of scouts comprising 150 to 200 soldiers. The rectangular fort covered an area of 78 by 93 metres. Surrounded by a ditch, it had corner towers, four gates and inner buildings typical of Roman camps. The site is now an architectural park landscape. The defensive walls of the fort, the apse of the standards shrine and sections of walls of structures such as the commander's house and the stores building have been preserved. Remains of a thermal bath, or "balnearium", in front of the fort with a cold bath and a warm bath have also survived. Many artefacts from the Feldberg garrison are now housed in the reconstructed Fort of Saalburg near Bad Homburg vor der Höhe.

Römerkastell
Kleiner Feldberg
61479 Glashütten
www.schloesser-hessen.de/
de/roemerkastell-
kleiner-feldberg

RÖMERKASTELL KAPERSBURG, ROSBACH VOR DER HÖHE

ROMAN FORT OF KAPERSBURG, ROSBACH VOR DER HÖHE

Was andernorts der Landwirtschaft zum Opfer fiel, hat sich in den schützenden Wäldern des hessischen Taunus gut erhalten. Die militärischen Befestigungen der Römer wie die Kapersburg bei Rosbach vor der Höhe geben eine Vorstellung vom Limes in der Spätantike. Die einstigen Wach- und Kundschafterposten gehören heute zum UNESCO-Welterbe Grenzen des Römischen Reiches.

Römerkastell Kapersburg
61191 Ober-Rosbach
www.schloesser-hessen.de/
de/roemerkastell-kapersburg

Wie das Kastell Kleiner Feldberg war auch die westlich von Rosbach vor der Höhe gelegene Kapersburg einst Teil des Obergermanisch-Raetischen Limes, der auf 550 Kilometern zwischen Rhein und Donau die Grenze des Römischen Reiches befestigte.

Vom 1. bis 3. Jahrhundert war das Kastell Standort einer mobilen Einheit aus 150 bis 200 Kundschaftern mit angegliederter Reiterabteilung. Die Kapersburg maß 134 mal 122 Meter und war in Stein ausgebaut. Bis heute sind rund um das Kastell Wehrgräben sichtbar sowie auf der West- und Ostseite die Umfassungsmauer und Tore. Von den Gebäuden sind unter anderem Reste der Verwaltungsräume, der Getreidespeicher sowie einer Mannschaftsbaracke erhalten. Außerhalb lag ein Lagerdorf, von dem nur noch die Grundmauern des Badehauses zeugen, welches Soldaten und Bevölkerung gemeinsam nutzten.

Die erhaltenen Gebäudereste stammen aus verschiedenen Bauphasen, denn das Kastell wurde mehrfach erweitert. In seiner Spätzeit, im zweiten Drittel des 3. Jahrhunderts, ist auch der schleichende Rückzug der Römer vom Limes an den Resten ablesbar: Damals zog sich eine deutlich kleinere Truppe in die festungsartig ausgebaute Nordostecke des Lagers zurück.

A feature that in other places has fallen victim to agriculture has been well preserved in the protective forests of Hesse's Taunus mountain range. Rome's military fortifications such as the Fort of Kapersburg near Rosbach vor der Höhe give an insight into the Limes in Late Antiquity. The former guard and scouting posts today form part of UNESCO's World Heritage site "Frontiers of the Roman Empire".

Like the Fort of Kleiner Feldberg, the Fort of Kapersburg, situated to the west of Rosbach vor der Höhe, once formed part of the Upper German Raetian Limes, which served to fortify a 550-kilometre stretch of the border of the Roman Empire between the Rhine and Danube rivers.

From the first to the third centuries, the fort housed a mobile unit of 150 to 200 scouts with an attached cavalry unit. Measuring 134 by 122 metres, the Fort of Kapersburg was built of stone. Defensive ditches can still be seen around the fort today, along with the enclosure wall and gateways on the west and east sides. Examples of preserved buildings include remains of the administrative rooms, the grain store and a soldiers' barracks. A camp village was located outside the fort. Of this, only the foundations of the bath house, which was used by both the soldiers and the local population, remain.

The preserved buildings stem from various construction phases, as the fort underwent several extensions. The remains also bear witness to the gradual withdrawal of the Romans from the Limes in the fort's latter period in the second third of the third century. This was when a significantly smaller troop of soldiers withdrew to the fortified extended north-east corner of the camp.

RÖMERBRUNNEN KAICHEN

ROMAN WELL KAICHEN, KAICHEN

Der Brunnen liegt malerisch auf einer Anhöhe südwestlich des Dorfes Kaichen in der Wetterau. Einst gehörte er zu einem römischen Gutshof. Der Obergermanisch-Raetische Limes, die Außengrenze des Römischen Reiches, machte hier einen Bogen nach Norden, um die fruchtbaren Böden der Wetterau einzubeziehen, die die Lebensmittelversorgung der umliegenden Städte und Kastelle sicherstellten.

The well is picturesquely situated on a hill south-west of the village of Kaichen in the Wetterau floodplain and once belonged to a Roman estate. The Upper German Raetian Limes, the outer frontiers of the Roman Empire, turned to the north here so as to include the fertile soils of the Wetterau floodplain and thus ensure the supply of food to the surrounding towns and forts.

Der Ziehbrunnen liegt nahe an der heutigen Landstraße von Karben nach Heldenbergen, die der einstigen Römerstraße folgt. Bei Ausgrabungen im Jahr 1902 wurden die Grundmauern eines römischen Gutshofs ergraben, zu dem auch der Brunnen gehörte. Im Brunnenschacht fand man zwei tuskische Steinsäulen, die wohl einst den Eingang der Villa geschmückt hatten und die man nun auf den Brunnenrand stellte, mit einem Querbalken verband und mit einem kleinen Dach bekrönte. Den Ziehbrunnen muss man sich also ursprünglich etwas schlichter vorstellen, als er sich heute präsentiert. Der Brunnenschacht ist original – allerdings war er einst fast doppelt so tief. Für die Wetterau sind zahlreiche solcher Landgüter belegt, die häufig von verdienten ehemaligen römischen Legionären geführt wurden. Von hier aus erfolgte die landwirtschaftliche Versorgung der Siedlung in Heldenbergen, der Truppen des Limes und des Friedberger Kastells. Ebenso dürfte die ehemalige Stadt Nida (auf dem Gebiet des heutigen Frankfurt-Heddernheim) Lebensmittel aus dieser Gegend bezogen haben.

Römerbrunnen Kaichen
61194 Kaichen
www.schloesser-hessen.de/
de/roemerbrunnen-kaichen

The draw well is located close to the current country road between Karben and Heldenbergen, which follows the former Roman road. Excavations in 1902 unearthed the foundation walls of a Roman estate, which also included the well. Two Tuscan stone pillars, which probably once decorated the entrance to the villa, were found in the well's shaft. They were re-erected on the edge of the well, connected by a crossbeam and covered with a small roof. The draw well would thus originally have been somewhat plainer than it appears today. Although the well shaft is original, it was once almost twice as deep.

Numerous such estates are documented for the Wetterau floodplain and were often granted to deserving Roman legionnaires on completion of their service. The estate served to feed the population in Heldenbergen, the troops of the Limes and of the Fort at Friedberg. The town of Nida (in the area of what is today known as Frankfurt-Heddernheim) may also have obtained food from the estate.

WETTERAU, MARBURGER LAND UND VOGELSBERG

WETTERAU, MARBURGER LAND AND VOGELSBERG

FÜRSTENGRUFT BUTZBACH

THE FÜRSTENGRUFT PRINCELY CRYPT BUTZBACH

Zwischen 1620 und 1622 ließ sich Landgraf Philipp III. von Hessen-Butzbach (1581–1643) in der gotischen Markuskirche in Butzbach eine Gruft einrichten. Er war hochgelehrt und stand unter anderem mit Galileo Galilei (1564–1641/42) in Kontakt. Seine Grablege besticht durch die Qualität der Stuckreliefs mit einem bemerkenswerten Bildprogramm, das Philipp wohl selbst ersonnen hat.

Between 1620 and 1622, Landgrave Philipp III of Hesse-Butzbach (1581–1643) had a crypt built in the Gothic Markus Church in Butzbach. Philipp was very learned and corresponded with Galileo Galilei (1564–1641/42), among others. His burial place is notable due to the quality of the stucco reliefs with their remarkable series of images, which may even have been devised by Philipp himself.

Nach dem Tod seines Vaters, des Landgrafen Georg I. von Hessen-Darmstadt (1547–1596), erhielt Philipp die Stadt Butzbach mit einigen umliegenden Dörfern als Erbteil. Da er kinderlos blieb, erlosch die von ihm begründete Butzbacher Nebenlinie bereits mit seinem Tod 1643.

Unter dem südlichen Chor der Butzbacher Markuskirche ließ der Landgraf zwischen 1620 und 1622 eine Begräbnisstätte errichten. Dazu gehören ein oberirdisches Epitaph und eine Gruft, in der vier Personen beigesetzt sind: Philipp selbst, seine beiden Ehefrauen und sein Urgroßneffe Heinrich von Hessen-Darmstadt (1674–1741).

Die Bogen- und Gewölbefelder der Gruft zieren figürliche Reliefs mit biblischen Szenen und Zitaten aus dem Apostolischen Glaubensbekenntnis. Das Bildprogramm ist den Themen der Auferstehung und Erlösung gewidmet. Die Entwürfe für die Reliefs stammen wahrscheinlich von dem Frankfurter Maler Philipp Uffenbach (1566–1636).

Fürstengruft Butzbach
Kirchplatz 12
35510 Butzbach
www.schloesser-hessen.de/
de/fuerstengruft-butzbach

Following the death of his father, Land-grave George I of Hesse-Darmstadt (1547–1596), Philipp was granted the town of Butzbach with some surrounding villages as his inheritance. As Philipp had no children, the Butzbach collateral line expired on his death in 1643.

Between 1620 and 1622, the landgrave had a final resting place prepared beneath the south chancel of the Markus Church in Butzbach. This included an above-ground epitaph and a crypt in which four people are buried – Philipp himself, his two wives, and his great-grandnephew Heinrich of Hesse-Darmstadt (1674–1741).

The crypt's tympana and severies are adorned with figurative reliefs depicting biblical scenes and also inscriptions from the Apostolic Creed. The images are devoted to the subjects of resurrection and salvation. The designs for the reliefs probably originated from the Frankfurt painter Philipp Uffenbach (1566–1636).

BURGRUINE MÜNZENBERG

MÜNZENBERG CASTLE RUINS

Die unverkennbare Silhouette der Burgruine Münzenberg erhebt sich, von Weitem sichtbar, auf einem Basaltrücken über der Ebene. Mit ihren zwei mächtigen Bergfrieden, dem dazwischen aufragenden Giebel und den massiven, teils zinnenbewehrten Mauern erzählt sie noch als Ruine vom Machtanspruch mittelalterlicher Herrscher. Der Volksmund nennt sie liebevoll „Wetterauer Tintenfass".

◄ Wehrgang im Bereich des
romanischen Palas
Walk-walk in the Romanesque palas

Errichtet wurde die Burg Münzenberg Mitte des 12. Jahrhunderts unter der Ägide der Staufer, die damals die römisch-deutschen Könige und Kaiser stellten. Mit insgesamt zehn Burgen in der Wetterau sicherten sie ihren Anspruch auf das Land – unterstützt von lokalen Adeligen wie Kuno von Hagen-Arnsburg, dem Bauherrn der Burg Münzenberg.

Vom ersten Bauabschnitt sind heute der östliche und südliche Teil der inneren Ringmauer, der östliche Bergfried und der romanische Palas erhalten. Mit diesen Bauten entsprach die Anlage dem Ideal einer stauferzeitlichen Burg. 1255 starben die Münzenberger in

männlicher Linie aus. In der Folge lebten in der Burg unter anderem die Herren von Falkenstein, die um 1260 einen zweiten, gotischen Palas errichteten. Außerdem vollendeten sie die Ringmauer und den westlichen Bergfried.

Während des Dreißigjährigen Krieges (1618–1648) in weiten Teilen zerstört, wurde die Anlange nicht wieder in Stand gesetzt und verfiel seither zur Ruine. Noch heute zeigt die Münzenburg eindrucksvoll, dass sie zu den bedeutendsten romanischen Burganlagen Deutschlands zählt und bietet herrliche Ausblicke in die Landschaft.

Visible from afar, the distinctive silhouette of Münzenberg
Castle Ruins rises high up on a basalt ridge above the plain.
With its two imposing keeps, the tall gabled building between them and the huge walls, some of which include
battlements, the castle chronicles the desire for power amongst
medieval rulers even in its ruined state. The castle ruins
are often affectionately referred to locally as the Wetterauer
Tintenfass, or Wetterau Inkwell.

Burgruine Münzenberg
35516 Münzenberg
www.schloesser-hessen.de/
de/burgruine-muenzenberg

◀ Blick vom Ostturm in den Burghof
mit dem romanischen Palas links und
dem gotischen Palas rechts im Bild
*View from the eastern tower into
the castle courtyard including the
Romanesque Palas on the left and the
Gothic palace on the right*

Münzenberg Castle was built in the middle of the 12th century under the auspices of the Staufen dynasty, which provided the Holy Roman kings and emperors of the time. Supported by local nobles such as Kuno von Hagen-Arnsburg, lord of Münzenberg Castle, they secured their claim to the land with a total of ten castles in the Wetterau floodplain.

Of the first construction phase, the eastern and southern sections of the inner curtain wall, the eastern keep and the Romanesque great hall (representative hall) are preserved today. With these buildings, the complex attained the ideal of a Staufer-era castle. After the Münzenberg male lineage died out in 1255, the castle was subsequently inhabited by the lords of Falkenstein, among others. They built a second Gothic great hall around 1260. They also completed the curtain wall and the western keep. Large portions were destroyed during the Thirty Years War (1618–1648); the complex was never repaired and has since fallen to ruin. Even today, Münzenburg Castle impressively asserts its status as one of the most important Romanesque castle complexes in Germany and offers fabulous views of the landscape.

▶ Aufgang zum Ostturm
Staircase to the eastern tower

67

ADOLFSTURM UND ST. GEORGSBRUNNEN IN DER BURG FRIEDBERG

ADOLF'S TOWER AND THE ST GEORGE FOUNTAIN, FRIEDBERG CASTLE

Die Burg Friedberg in der Wetterau erstreckt sich über ein fast quadratisches Areal von 3,9 Hektar. Damit zählt die einst reichsunmittelbare Burg zu den größten Anlagen ihrer Art in Deutschland. Adolfsturm und St. Georgsbrunnen sind Zeugen zweier sehr unterschiedlicher historischer Epochen in der höchst spannenden Geschichte der Burganlage.

Burg Friedberg
In der Burg
61169 Friedberg
www.schloesser-hessen.de/
de/adolfsturm

Ende des 12. Jahrhunderts gegründet, genoss die Burg Friedberg über viele Jahrhunderte hinweg den Status einer unmittelbar den römisch-deutschen Königen und Kaisern unterstellten Reichsburg. Die Burggrafschaft war von Burgmannen besiedelt und verfügte über ein eigenes Territorium sowie besondere Privilegien.

Die erhaltenen Befestigungsanlagen stammen zum Großteil aus dem 14. Jahrhundert. Dazu gehört auch der zinnenbesetzte, über 50 Meter hohe Adolfsturm am Nordtor. Seit 1347 überragt er einen der zwei Hauptzufahrtswege in die Burg. Der zentrale Spitzhelm und die vier Seitentürmchen sind Zutaten aus dem Ende des 19. Jahrhunderts. Im 17. und 18. Jahrhundert traten die repräsentativen Funktionen der Burg in den Vordergrund mit zusätzlicher Bautätigkeit. Aus dieser Zeit stammt ein von Johann Philipp Wörrishofer entworfener Springbrunnen aus Mainsandstein. In der Mitte des 1738 installierten Brunnens erhebt sich die Kopie der Figur des heiligen Georg, der den Drachen erlegt. Entworfen hat sie der Mainzer Bildhauer Burkhard Zamels (um 1690–1757). Das Original befindet sich heute im Friedberger Wetterau-Museum.

Friedberg Castle in the Wetterau floodplain extends over an almost square-shaped area of 3.9 hectares, making the castle, which was once directly subordinate to the Holy Roman Empire, one of the largest complexes of its type in Germany. Adolf's Tower and the St George Fountain testify to two very different historical periods in the fascinating history of the castle complex.

Founded at the end of the 12th century, for many hundreds of years Friedberg Castle enjoyed the status of an imperial castle that was directly subordinate to Holy Roman kings and emperors. The cooperatively organised burgraviate was inhabited by a knightly militia ("Burgmannen") and had its own territory and special privileges.

The preserved fortifications mostly date from the 14th century. These fortifications include Adolf's Tower, which is over 50 metres high and is located at the north gate. Encircled by ramparts, it has guarded one of the two main entrances to the castle since 1347. The central helm roof and four side towers were added at the end of the 19th century.

Additional building work in the 17th and 18th centuries brought the castle's representative functions to the fore. A water fountain designed by Johann Philipp Wörrishofer and made of Main sandstone stems from this period. The centre of the fountain, which was installed in 1738, contains a copy of a statue of St. George slaying the dragon. It was designed by the Mainz sculptor Burkhard Zamels (around 1690–1757). The original is today housed in Friedberg's Wetterau Museum.

JUNKER-HANSEN-TURM, NEUSTADT

JUNKER-HANSEN TOWER, NEUSTADT

Mit über zwölf Metern Durchmesser und einer Gesamthöhe von fast 50 Metern gilt der gotische Junker-Hansen-Turm heute als größter erhaltener Fachwerkrundbau weltweit mit eigenem Eintrag im Guinness-Buch der Rekorde. Als südöstliche Bastion einer neuen Stadtbefestigung, die nie fertiggestellt wurde, ist er heute das Wahrzeichen des hessischen Neustadt.

Junker-Hansen-Turm
Ritterstraße
35279 Neustadt
www.schloesser-hessen.de/
de/junker-hansen-turm

Errichtet wurde der Turm 1480 bis 1483 vom landgräflichen Baumeister Hans Jakob von Ettlingen (um 1440–1507). Auftrag- und Namensgeber war der hessische Hofmeister Junker Hans von Dörnberg (1427–1506), dem Landgraf Heinrich III. von Hessen (1440–1483) die Stadt verpfändet hatte. Geplant war eine gewaltige Festungsanlage, von der jedoch nur der Süd-West-Trakt sowie der Turm vollendet wurden. Im Junker-Hansen-Turm verbinden sich Wehr- und Wohncharakter mit den hohen Repräsentationsansprüchen Dörnbergs. Dieser hatte mit Hans Jakob von Ettlingen einen der führenden Festungsbaumeister seiner Zeit für sein Projekt gewonnen. Im Inneren führt eine steinerne Spindeltreppe in den Turmschaft mit je 3,50 Meter hohen Fachwerkgeschossen, die getrennt verzimmert wurden. Die hier angewandte Bauweise mit komplex ineinander verschränktem Gebälk und das steil aufragende Schieferdach mit den vier Erkertürmchen zeigen die hohe Kunstfertigkeit der Handwerker.

Dank der Wiederherstellung der historisch belegten Schieferabdeckung an der Wetterseite sowie der aufwendigen Neueindeckung des Daches präsentiert sich der Turm heute weitestgehend in seinem ursprünglichen Erscheinungsbild.

With a diameter of over twelve metres and a total height of almost 50 metres, the Gothic Junker-Hansen Tower is today the world's largest preserved half-timbered circular building and has its own entry in the **Guinness Book of Records**. Built as the south-eastern bastion of new fortifications (which were never completed) for Neustadt, the tower now forms the landmark of this Hessian town.

The tower was constructed from 1480 to 1483 by landgraviate builder Hans Jakob von Ettlingen (around 1440–1507). It was commissioned by and named after Hessian Hofmeister Junker Hans von Dörnberg (1427–1506), to whom Landgrave Heinrich III of Hesse-Marburg had pledged the city. Although huge fortifications were planned, only the south-western section and the tower were completed.

The Junker-Hansen Tower combines defensive and domestic features with Dörnberg's exacting demands for a prestigious structure. In Hans Jakob von Ettlingen, he secured one of the leading fortification engineers of the time for his project. Inside the tower, a stone spiral staircase in the tower's shaft leads to half-timbered storeys, each 3.5 metres high, which had separate timber supports. The building technique used here with complex interlocking timberwork and the steeply rising slated roof with four corner turrets evidence the great skills of the craftsmen.

Following the restoration of the historical slate covering on the windward side and the extensive recovering of the roof, the tower now appears largely as it originally looked.

ELISABETHBRUNNEN SCHRÖCK BEI MARBURG

THE ELISABETH FOUNTAIN, SCHRÖCK, MARBURG

In einen mit Buchen bewachsenen Berghang eingebettet, beeindruckt der Elisabethbrunnen wenige Kilometer östlich von Marburg durch seine mächtige Sandsteinfassade im Renaissancestil. Gewidmet ist der Brunnen nahe dem Marburger Stadtteil Schröck Landgräfin Elisabeth von Thüringen (1207–1231), die bereits vier Jahre nach ihrem Tod zur Heiligen erhoben wurde.

Set into a hillside covered in beech trees, the Elisabeth Fountain with its imposing Renaissance-style sandstone façade is an impressive sight just a few kilometres east of Marburg. The fountain, which is close to the Marburg district of Schröck, is dedicated to Landgravine Elisabeth of Thuringia (1207–1231), who was canonised just four years after her death.

Elisabeth von Thüringen verbrachte ihre letzten Lebensjahre in Marburg, wo sie in Armut lebte, sich für Kranke und Bedürftige aufopferte und wohl zahlreiche Wunder bewirkte. Laut Legende soll sie sich auch häufiger an der später nach ihr benannten Quelle erfrischt haben.
Als Ludwig IV. von Hessen-Marburg (1537–1604) die Quelle 1596 fassen ließ, knüpfte er damit ein Band zwischen seiner jungen, erst 1567 durch Erbteilung entstandenen Landgrafschaft und einer Heiligen, die zudem als Stammmutter des Hauses Hessens gilt.

Vor dem lichten Buchenwald wirkt die etwa sieben Meter hohe Sandsteinfassade nahezu monumental. Sie wurde nach Plänen des Hofbaumeisters Ebert Baldewein (1525–1593) errichtet, der dabei antike Formensprache aufgriff. Unten rahmen vier dorische Säulen einen Rundbogen, durch den man in die Brunnenstube gelangt. Der bekrönende Giebel mit den landgräflichen Wappen sitzt auf einem zweiten, von ionischen Säulen getragenen Geschoss. Die dort angebrachte lateinische Inschrift preist die umgebende Natur, erzählt von der heiligen Elisabeth und den Geburtstagsfesten, die Ludwig IV. hier feierte.

Zum Elisabethbrunnen
35043 Marburg, Schröck
www.schloesser-hessen.de/
de/elisabethbrunnen

Elisabeth of Thuringia spent the final years of her life in Marburg. Living in poverty, she sacrificed herself to looking after the sick and needy and is said to have performed numerous miracles. According to legend, she also often refreshed herself at the spring, which was later dedicated to her.

When Landgrave Ludwig IV of Hesse-Marburg (1537–1604) had the source contained in 1596, he forged a bond between his young Landgraviate (which had only been created in 1567 as a result of a testamentary partition) and a saint who was also considered the ancestress of the House of Hesse.

The sandstone façade standing around seven metres tall appears almost monumental in front of the thinly wooded beech forest. It was built according to plans by court architect Ebert Baldewein (1525–1593), who styled it based on the design language of antiquity. On the ground floor, four Doric columns frame a rounded arch which forms the entrance to the water chamber. The crowning gable is decorated with the landgraviate's coats of arms and sits atop a second floor supported by ionic columns. The Latin inscription on the second floor praises the surrounding nature, tells of Saint Elisabeth, and recalls the birthday feasts celebrated here by Ludwig IV.

GALGEN VON HOPF-MANNSFELD, LAUTERTAL

THE GALLOWS OF HOPFMANNSFELD, LAUTERTAL

Die einstige Hinrichtungsstätte des Hopfmannsfelder Gerichts zählt zu den außergewöhnlichsten Kulturdenkmälern in der Obhut der Staatlichen Schlösser und Gärten Hessen. Die steinernen Überreste eines 1707 errichteten Galgens zeugen von einer Strafpraxis, die erst mit der Aufklärung Ende des 18. Jahrhunderts zunehmend in Verruf geriet.

The former execution ground of the Hopfmannsfeld Court is among the most unusual cultural monuments in the care of State Palaces and Gardens Hesse. The stone remains of gallows built in 1707 testify to punishment measures that only fell into increasing disrepute with the Enlightenment at the end of the 18th century.

Zwischen Hopfmannsfeld und Lautertal stehen zwei Sandsteinsäulen am Wegesrand. Es sind die Reste eines 1707 errichteten Galgens. Oben haben sie Aussparungen, in denen einst ein hölzerner Querbalken lag, um daran Strick oder Kette zu befestigen.

Solche Richtstätten befanden sich meist außerhalb der Ortschaften an auffälliger Stelle, auf einem Hügel oder wie hier an einer Wegkreuzung. Die Erhängten wurden für alle Passanten sichtbar am Galgen belassen und nicht begraben. Einst gab es zahlreiche Hinrichtungsstätten dieser Art, denn jedes Gericht musste als Zeichen seiner Strafgewalt einen Galgen aufweisen, der häufig an den Gemarkungsgrenzen stand, um den Geltungsbereich des Rechtsbezirks zu betonen. Vor allem in ländlichen Regionen haben sich einige erhalten, in Hessen zum Beispiel der Stockhäuser Galgen sowie weitere bei Steinheim (Ortsteil von Hanau), Münzenberg, Pfungstadt und Beerfelden.

Ob jemals ein Delinquent am Hopfmannsfelder Galgen hingerichtet wurde, ist nicht belegt.

Galgen von Hopfmannsfeld
Alte Frankfurter Fahrstraße
36369 Lautertal-
Hopfmannsfeld
www.schloesser-hessen.de/
de/galgen-hopfmannsfeld

Two sandstone pillars stand at the road-side between Hopfmannsfeld and Lautertal. These are the remains of a gallows erected in 1707. The tops of the pillars contain notches for holding a wooden crossbeam to which rope or chain could be attached.

Such places of execution were mainly located at prominent sites outside of settlements – on a hill or at a crossroads, as here. The people who had been hanged were not buried, but left on the gallows for all passers-by to see. Numerous such execution places existed in the past as

each court needed to have a set of gallows to demonstrate its penal authority. These gallows often stood at the boundaries between districts in order to mark the territory of an individual jurisdiction. Some gallows have been preserved, especially in rural regions. Examples in Hesse include the Stockhaus gallows and others at Steinheim (a district of Hanau), Münzenberg, Pfungstadt and Beerfelden.

There is no documentary evidence proving whether a criminal was ever executed at the Hopfmannsfeld gallows.

IM NORDEN HESSENS

IN NORTH HESSE

HAFENBECKEN BAD KARLSHAFEN

BAD KARLSHAFEN HARBOUR BASIN

Das Hafenbecken in Bad Karlshafen am Zusammenfluss von Weser und Diemel ganz im Norden Hessens ist das Relikt eines ehrgeizigen Vorhabens: Landgraf Karl von Hessen-Kassel (1654–1730) plante eine Wasserstraße, die das damalige Sieburg (1717 zu seinen Ehren in Carlshaven umbenannt) mit Kassel verbinden und weiter bis zur Lahn verlaufen sollte.

The harbour basin in Bad Karlshafen at the confluence of the Weser and Diemel rivers in the far north of Hesse is a relic of an ambitious project: Landgrave Karl of Hesse-Kassel (1654–1730) wanted to create a canal, entirely on the territory of the Landgraviate of Hesse-Kassel, to connect the town previously known as Sieburg (which was renamed Carlshaven in his honour in 1717) with Kassel and then continue on to the Lahn River.

Ab 1710 forcierte Karl sein Kanalprojekt, und kurz danach begannen auch der Bau des Hafenbeckens in Bad Karlshafen sowie der Ausbau der Stadt zu einer barocken Anlage. Die Beweggründe des Landesherrn waren wirtschaftliche: Über den geplanten Kanal hätte er den natürlichen Wasserweg über Weser und Fulda in seine Hauptstadt Kassel abgekürzt, aber vor allem den Umweg über das Fürstentum Braunschweig-Wolfenbüttel und damit auch die Zahlung von Zöllen vermieden.
Dies war umso wichtiger, weil die erst 1699 unter dem Namen Sieburg gegründete Stadt das Zentrum hessischer Tuchproduktion war. Karl hatte hier den protestantischen Hugenotten Zuflucht gewährt, die von Ludwig XIV. (1638–1715) in Frankreich verfolgt wurden. Die exzellenten Kenntnisse der Glaubensflüchtlinge in der Tuchproduktion verhalfen der Stadt zu Wohlstand.
Das Kanalprojekt endete 1730 mit dem Tod des Landgrafen – 19 Kilometer waren fertiggestellt. In den 1930er-Jahren wurde das Hafenbecken durch den Bau einer Straße von der Weser abgeschnitten, ist aber seit 2019 wieder für Schiffe erreichbar. So ankern heute im beschaulichen Hafen kleine Yachten und Freizeitboote vor der eindrucksvollen Kulisse des barocken Rathauses.

Hafenbecken
Bad Karlshafen
34385 Bad Karlshafen
www.schloesser-hessen.de/
de/hafen-bad-karlshafen

Karl pressed ahead with his canal project from 1710, and the construction of the harbour basin in Bad Karlshafen, and the expansion of the town into a Baroque complex also commenced shortly thereafter. The landgrave was motivated by commercial interests, as his planned canal would have shortened the natural waterway via the Weser and Fulda rivers to his capital of Kassel. But more importantly, it would have avoided the detour through the Principality of Braunschweig-Wolfenbüttel and so also avoided the payment of customs duties.

This was all the more important because the town, which had only been founded in 1699 initially under the name of Sieburg, was the centre of Hessian cloth production. Karl had granted the protestant Huguenots, persecuted by Louis XIV (1638–1715) in France, refuge in the town. And the skills of the religious refugees in the art of cloth production had helped the town to prosper.

The canal project ended on the landgrave's death in 1730, with 19 kilometres completed. In the 1930s, the harbour basin was cut off from the River Weser by the construction of a road. However, it has been accessible to boats again since 2019, with small yachts and leisure craft today mooring in front of the impressive backdrop of the Baroque town hall.

SCHLOSS SPANGENBERG

SPANGENBERG PALACE

Schloss Spangenberg, 1235 erstmals urkundlich erwähnt, liegt auf einem bewaldeten Hügel über dem nordhessischen Ort gleichen Namens. Das nach Zerstörungen des Zweiten Weltkriegs wieder aufgebaute Schloss ist heute ein anschauliches Beispiel für eine gut befestigte Burganlage der Frühen Neuzeit. Ein tiefer Graben umgibt das Gebäudeensemble, das nur über eine Brücke erreichbar ist.

Die an der Handelsstraße zwischen Frankfurt und Leipzig gelegene Burg war einst Sitz der aus Thüringen stammenden Herren von Treffurt. Das Aussehen der mittelalterlichen Höhenburg ist nicht überliefert, der Lebenswandel ihrer Bewohner:innen hingegen schon: Die in einer Familienfehde zerstrittenen Treffurter waren seit dem frühen 14. Jahrhundert berüchtigte Raubritter. 1350 verkauften sie die Burg samt Amt und Stadt Spangenberg für 8.000 Mark Silber an den hessischen Landgrafen Heinrich II. (vor 1302–1376). Seitdem wurde sie in der wald- und wildreichen Gegend vor allem als Jagdschloss genutzt.

Die Landgrafen bauten die Anlage aus, wobei sie insbesondere die Befestigungsanlagen verstärkten. Damals entstand auch der tiefe Graben um das Schloss. Vor allem Landgraf Wilhelm IV. (1532–1592), dem Begründer der Linie Hessen-Kassel, verdankt das Schloss seine heutige Gestalt.

Bis ins 20. Jahrhundert blieb Schloss Spangenberg dank seiner Wehrhaftigkeit weitgehend unversehrt. Nach einem Bombenangriff im Zweiten Weltkrieg brannte die Anlage ab, wurde aber in den 1950er-Jahren umfassend rekonstruiert. Heute sind im Schloss ein Jagdmuseum und ein Hotel mit Landgastwirtschaft untergebracht.

Spangenberg Palace, first mentioned in records in 1235, lies on a wooded hill above the north Hessian locality of the same name. Rebuilt after being destroyed in the Second World War, the palace is now a fine example of a strongly fortified castle complex of the early modern era. A deep ditch surrounds the ensemble of buildings, which can only be accessed via a bridge.

Located on the trade route between Frankfurt and Leipzig, the castle was once the seat of the Treffurt family, who originated from Thuringia. Although the appearance of the medieval hilltop castle has been lost to time, the lifestyle of its inhabitants is well documented: the Treffurt family became embroiled in a family feud and were notorious robber barons from the early 14th century. In 1350 they sold the castle including the title and the town of Spangenberg for 8,000 silver marks to the Hessian landgrave Heinrich II (pre 1302–1376). After this date, it was mainly used as a hunting lodge for the surrounding game-rich, forested area.

The landgraves undertook a process of expansion, which in particular included strengthening the complex's fortifications. They also created the deep ditch around the palace. The palace owes its current design to Landgrave William IV (1532–1592) in particular, who founded the Hesse–Kassel line.

Spangenberg Palace's defensive strength ensured it remained largely intact until the 20th century. The complex burned down following a bomb attack during the Second World War, but was extensively rebuilt in the 1950s. The castle now houses a hunting museum and a hotel with a country restaurant.

Schloss Spangenberg
Zum Schloss 1
34286 Spangenberg
www.schloesser-hessen.de/
de/schloss-spangenberg

BURGRUINE FELSBERG
FELSBERG CASTLE RUINS

Die Burgruine sitzt hoch oben auf einem Basaltkegel über der Stadt Felsberg in Nordhessen. Prägend für ihr heutiges Aussehen ist der im 15. Jahrhundert unter den hessischen Landgrafen ausgebaute, zweigeteilte Bergfried, ein sogenannter Butterfassturm, bei dem der obere Teil schmaler als der untere ist. Für die Landgrafen war die Burg als Stützpunkt gegen Mainz strategisch wichtig.

Bereits 1060 ist der Bau einer Burg über dem Edertal urkundlich bezeugt. Die Bauherren und Amtsgrafen von Felsberg lebten nachweislich bis 1286 auf der Burg. Im 13. Jahrhundert gehörte die Anlage zunächst zur Landgrafschaft Thüringen, 1247 fiel sie an die hessischen Landgrafen, die im 14. Jahrhundert die Wehranlagen ausbauen ließen. Im Kampf mit Kurmainz um die Vorherrschaft in der Region ließ Landgraf Ludwig I. (1402–1458) im 15. Jahrhundert schließlich den Bergfried erhöhen und umbauen. Ludwig war es auch, der den Alchemisten Klaus von Urbach auf die Burg holte, von dem er sich erhoffte, er könne Gold herstellen – was ihm leider nicht gelang.

Später diente die Burg verschiedenen hessischen Landgräfinnen als Witwensitz, darunter auch Anna zu Mecklenburg (1485–1525), der Mutter Philipps des Großmütigen (1504–1567). Nach dem frühen Tod ihres Ehemannes gelang es ihr, gegen den Willen der hessischen Landstände die Regentschaft für den noch unmündigen Philipp durchzusetzen.

Ab 1550 trug man die Burg nach und nach ab. Erhalten haben sich der Bergfried sowie Reste der Umfassungs- und Zwingermauern mit Türmen. In der ehemaligen Burgkapelle befindet sich heute ein kleines Museum.

The castle ruins sit on a basalt rock formation high above the town of Felsberg in North Hesse. Their current appearance is shaped by the two-part keep, which was extended in the 15th century under the Hessian landgraves and which is known as a butter churn tower, where the upper section is slimmer than the lower part. The castle was strategically important for the landgraves as it served as a bulwark against Mainz.

Burgruine Felsberg
Burgstraße
34587 Felsberg
www.schloesser-hessen.de/
de/burgruine-felsberg

The construction of a castle above the Eder Valley was mentioned in records as early as 1060. According to documents, the castle's builders, the Counts of Felsberg, lived in the castle until 1286. In the 13th century, the castle initially belonged to the Landgraviate of Thuringia. In 1247, however, it fell to the Hessian landgraves, who had the fortifications extended in the 14th century. Then, during the conflict with the Electorate of Mainz for domination in the region, Landgrave Ludwig I (1402–1458) had the keep extended and remodelled in the 15th century. It was also Ludwig who summoned the alchemist Klaus von Urbach to the castle in the forlorn hope that he would be able to produce gold.

The castle later served various Hessian landgravines as a widow's residence, including Anna zu Mecklenburg (1485–1525), the mother of Philipp the Magnanimous (1504–1567). After the early death of her husband, she succeeded, against the will of the Hessian "Landstände" (political representatives of the estates of the realm in the German Empire), in securing the regency for Philipp, who was still under age.

The castle fell into gradual disrepair from 1550. The keep and the remains of the surrounding and fortified walls with towers have been preserved. A small museum is now housed in the castle's former chapel.

BURG FÜRSTENECK, EITERFELD

FÜRSTENECK CASTLE, EITERFELD

Die bei Eiterfeld in der Rhön gelegene Burg Fürsteneck ist eine spätmittelalterliche Gründung der Fürstäbte von Fulda, zu deren Einflussgebiet die Region um Fürsteneck bereits seit 845 zählte. Die 1330 erstmals erwähnte Burg diente über viele Jahrhunderte der Sicherung der Fuldaer Territorien. Heute beherbergt die Burg eine Akademie für berufliche und musisch-kulturelle Weiterbildung.

Betritt man die Anlage durch das schmale Burgtor, so eröffnet sich ein fast rechteckiger Hof, der von Bauten aus verschiedenen Jahrhunderten umstanden ist. Von der ursprünglichen Wehranlage sind der quadratische Bergfried, allerdings nicht in voller Höhe, die Ringmauer sowie einige Wohnbauten erhalten. Ein Blickfang ist der dreigeschossige, in seinem Kern spätgotische Wohnbau. Die Zwingeranlage samt Wehrgang und kleiner Bastion stammt vermutlich aus dem 16. Jahrhundert.

Nach ihrer Zerstörung im Dreißigjährigen Krieg (1618–1648) baute Fürstabt Adalbert von Schleifras (1650–1714) die Burg ab 1708 wieder auf. Davon zeugt noch heute sein Wappen über dem Türrahmen des Herrenhauses. In der Folge diente die nun schlossartige Anlage unter anderem als Sommerresidenz der Fuldaer Äbte, bis sie 1802 im Zuge der Säkularisation kirchlicher Besitzungen in Staatshand überging.

Unter dem Architekten Otto Bartning (1883–1959), welcher dem Bauhaus nahestand, wurde die Anlage in den 1950er-Jahren umfassend instandgesetzt und unter weitgehender Wahrung der originalen Bausubstanz zu einem Ort der Erwachsenenbildung umgebaut.

Fürsteneck Castle near Eiterfeld in the Rhön region is a late-medieval establishment of the Prince Abbots of Fulda, whose area of influence included the region around Fürsteneck as early as 845. The castle, which was first mentioned in records in 1330, served to secure the Fuldaer territories for many centuries. The castle is now home to an academy for professional, musical and cultural continuing education.

Burg Fürsteneck
Am Schlossgarten 3
36132 Eiterfeld
www.schloesser-hessen.de/
de/burg-fuersteneck

Entering the complex through the narrow castle gate, visitors pass into an almost rectangular courtyard, which is surrounded by buildings from various centuries. Of the original defensive system, the square keep is preserved (although not in its full height), as are the curtain wall and some residential buildings. The three-storey mainly late-Gothic residential building is a particular highlight. The ward complex including wall-walk and small bastion is said to date from the 16th century.
After it was destroyed during the Thirty Years' War (1618–1648), Prince Abbot Adalbert von Schleifras (1650–1714) re-

built the castle from 1708. His coat of arms above the door frame of the manor house bears evidence of this today. The complex, which now resembled a palace, subsequently served as a summer residence for the Abbots of Fulda, until it was transferred to state ownership in 1802 during the secularisation of ecclesiastical property.
In the 1950s, the complex underwent extensive renovations under the architect Otto Bartning (1883–1959), who was close to the Bauhaus movement. Preserving much of the building's original substance, the castle was transformed into an adult education establishment.

VON NORD NACH SÜD – KLÖSTER, KIRCHEN UND EINE KAISERPFALZ

FROM NORTH TO SOUTH – MONASTERIES, CHURCHES AND AN IMPERIAL PALACE

KLOSTER CORNBERG
CORNBERG MONASTERY

Die Gründung des Klosters Cornberg vor über 700 Jahren erfolgte vermutlich auf Betreiben der Burgmannen der benachbarten Boyneburg. Denn das Kloster sollte nicht zuletzt den ledig gebliebenen Frauen der Adelsfamilien ein Auskommen sichern. 1393 lebten nachweislich 28 Benediktinerinnen im Kloster, deren Unterhalt großzügige Schenkungen und Mitgiften sicherten.

Dating back over 700 years, Cornberg Monastery was probably founded at the instigation of the knightly militia ("Burgmannen") of neighbouring Boyneburg. The main purpose of the monastery was to secure a livelihood for single women of noble families. Records show that in 1393 the monastery housed 28 Benedictine nuns, whose upkeep secured generous donations and dowries.

Kloster Cornberg
Am Steinbruch 1
36219 Cornberg
www.schloesser-hessen.de/
de/kloster-cornberg

Das Benediktinerinnenkloster Cornberg ging aus dem Beginenhaus in Bubenbach hervor, einer christlichen Frauengemeinschaft ohne Ordensgelübde und Klausur, die sich 1230 der benediktinischen Reichsabtei Hersfeld unterstellt hatte. Zwischen 1292 und 1296 siedelten die Nonnen in das geschützt gelegene Tal von Cornberg über.
Die schlichten Klostergebäude sind aus dem charakteristisch gebänderten Cornberger Sandstein errichtet. Sie ordnen sich um einen quadratischen Hof. Nördlich liegt die kurz vor 1300 erbaute Kirche, ein einschiffiger Bau mit Glockenturm, mit einer heute noch erhaltenen Nonnenempore.

1526 wurde das Kloster im Zuge der Reformation aufgelöst und den hessischen Landgrafen übergeben. Der Gebäudekomplex samt umliegender Ländereien war seitdem ein landwirtschaftliches Hofgut, und seit 1834 bis 1964 Staatsdomäne. In der zweiten Hälfte des 20. Jahrhunderts erfolgte der Abriss der ruinösen Wirtschafts- und Wohngebäude und in den 1990er-Jahren eine aufwendige Sanierung der gotischen Klosteranlage, die danach ihrer neuen Nutzung als Kulturbühne, Hotel und Bürgerhaus sowie Museum zugeführt wurde.

Cornberg Benedictine Monastery developed from the Beguines house in Bubenbach, a Christian community of women without religious vows or cloister which had submitted itself to the Benedictine imperial abbey of Hersfeld in 1230. Between 1292 and 1296 the nuns relocated to the sheltered Cornberg Valley.

The unpretentious monastery buildings are built from Cornberg sandstone with its characteristic banding, and are arranged around a square courtyard. To the north lies the single-nave church that was built shortly before 1300. It has a bell tower and a nun's gallery, which is still preserved today.

In 1526 the monastery was disbanded during the Reformation and handed over to the Hessian landgraves. The building complex and its surrounding lands then became an agricultural estate, and a state domain from 1834 to 1964. The ruined farmyard and residential buildings were demolished in the second half of the 20th century. The Gothic monastery complex was extensively renovated in the 1990s and subsequently converted to its new use as a cultural venue, hotel, community centre and museum.

STIFTSRUINE BAD HERSFELD

BAD HERSFELD COLLEGIATE CHURCH RUINS

Die Stiftskirche gehörte einst zur mächtigen Benediktinerabtei Hersfeld. Die größte romanische Kirchenruine
nördlich der Alpen ist heute insbesonere als Spielstätte
der Bad Hersfelder Festspiele bekannt.

▼ Die Ansicht des Ostchores mit
einer der kleinen Apsiden
*View of the east choir with one of
the small apses*

Jedes Jahr im Sommer pilgern Theaterbegeisterte nach Bad Hersfeld, wo sie zwischen den ehrwürdigen Mauern der Stiftsruine ein atmosphärisch einmaliger Kulturgenuss erwartet. Doch ein populäres Ziel war der mächtige Bau bereits knapp tausend Jahre früher: Damals war Hersfeld Missionszentrum und zog Scharen von Pilgern an, die am Grab des heiligen Wigbert (um 670 – um 732) und des Klostergründers und Mainzer Erzbischofs Lullus (um 710–786) beteten.

Ein erster Bau entstand nach der Gründung der Abtei 769, dem drei weitere folgten. Der letzte, bis heute erhaltene Bau wurde 1038 begonnen. Vom einstigen Mittelschiff der dreischiffigen Säulenbasilika zeugen nur noch einige Säulenbasen. Die erhaltenen Außenmauern geben jedoch einen imposanten Eindruck von der Architektur des 11. Jahrhunderts.

Im Siebenjährigen Krieg (1756–1763) stark beschädigt, diente die Anlage in der Folge als Steinbruch, und erst mit dem 19. Jahrhundert begannen Schutzmaßnahmen. Unmittelbar neben der Stiftsruine ist von der einstigen Klosteranlage auch der Katharinenturm erhalten, in dem die berühmte, 1038 gegossene Lullusglocke, die älteste datierte Glocke Deutschlands, immer noch ihren Dienst tut.

Stiftsruine Bad Hersfeld
Im Stift 6
36251 Bad Hersfeld
www.schloesser-hessen.de/
de/stiftsruine-bad-hersfeld

The collegiate church once belonged to the powerful Benedictine abbey of Hersfeld. Today, the largest Roman church ruins north of the Alps are especially famous as the venue for the Bad Hersfeld Festival.

▲ Blick in den Ostchor und die Krypta
View of the east choir and the crypt

▼ Blick vom Ostchor in den Westchor
View from the east choir to the west choir

▶ Figürliche Bauplastik mit der Darstellung eines Mönchs
Architectural sculpture with depiction of a monk

Every summer, theatre enthusiasts make a pilgrimage to Bad Hersfeld, where they can sit among the sacred walls of the collegiate church ruins and soak up a unique cultural experience. However, the huge structure was already a popular destination around a thousand years ago, when Hersfeld was a missionary centre attracting pilgrims wishing to pray at the grave of Saint Wigbert (around 670 to around 732) and of the monastery's founder and Archbishop of Mainz, Lullus (around 710–786).

A first structure was built on the site following the founding of the monastery in 769. Three further buildings followed, each bigger than the previous. The last building, which has been preserved to the present day, was started in 1038 in the form of a three-nave basilica. Although only a few column bases of the middle nave remain, the preserved external walls ensure that the ruins offer an authentic impression of 11th-century architecture.

Heavily damaged during the Seven Years' War (1756–1763), the complex then served as a quarry, with preservation measures only commencing during the 19th century. In addition to the collegiate church ruins, the Catherine Tower, which once formed part of the monastery complex, is still preserved and houses the famous Lullus Bell. Cast in 1038, it is the oldest datable bell in Germany and is still in working order.

PROPSTEI JOHANNESBERG, FULDA

JOHANNESBERG PROVOSTRY BUILDINGS, FULDA

Die Propstei Johannesberg blickt auf eine lange Geschichte zurück. Gegründet im 9. Jahrhundert als Nebenkloster der Abtei Fulda, war sie seit dem 17. Jahrhundert Propstei und nach der Säkularisation der kirchlichen Güter Staatsdomäne. Heute beherbergt das barocke Gebäudeensemble mit teilweise rekonstruierter Gartenanlage ein Fortbildungszentrum für Handwerk und Denkmalpflege.

▲ Treppenanlage zwischen erster
und zweiter Terrasse
*Steps between the first and second
terraces*

◄ Blick auf das Propsteischloss
und die Gartenanlage
*View to the provostry palace and
the gardens*

Bereits 811 ließ das Fuldaer Benedikti-
nerkloster wenige Kilometer südlich
der Abtei in den Fuldaauen einen ersten Kirchenbau errichten. Unter Abt
Rabanus Maurus (um 780–856) erfolgte
die Erhebung zum Nebenkloster. In
der Folge erlebte die Anlage mehrere
Um- und Neubauten.
Mit dem Dreißigjährigen Krieg (1618–
1648) endete das mönchische Leben in
Johannesberg. Das einstige Kloster
verwaltete den umfangreichen Grund-
besitz fortan als Propstei. Bereits Ende
des 17. Jahrhunderts erfolgte ein Umbau der Kirche im barocken Stil, die

übrige Anlage geht im Wesentlichen
auf die Amtszeit von Conrad von Mengersen (1677–1753, ab 1715 Propst)
zurück, der sie nach den Plänen des
fürstäbtlichen Hofbaumeisters Andrea
Gallasini (1681–1766) umgestalten ließ.
Es entstand ein neuer fürstlicher Wohn-
trakt, der sogenannte „Rote Bau".
Die ebenfalls unter Conrad von Mengersen geplante, nach Osten zur Fulda
hin ausgerichtete Gartenanlage gliedert
sich in eine obere große Terrasse mit
zwei Eckpavillons, Brunnen und skulp-
turalem Schmuck sowie zwei weitere
Terrassen.

The Johannesberg Provostry Buildings have a long history. Founded in the 9th century as a subsidiary monastery of Fulda Abbey, the complex became provostry buildings in the 17th century and subsequently a state domain following the secularisation of ecclesiastical property. Today, the Baroque building complex with partly restored gardens is used as a training centre for crafts and the preservation of historical monuments.

▼ Deckengemälde im nordöstlichen Eckzimmer mit Aurora, der Göttin der Morgenröte
Ceiling fresco in the northeastern corner room: Aurora, goddess of dawn

▲ Steinskulptur in der Gartenanlage
Stone sculpture in the gardens

Probstei Johannesberg
Propsteischloss 2
36041 Fulda
www.schloesser-hessen.de/
de/propstei-johannesberg

As early as 811, Fulda Benedictine Abbey had a first church built a few kilometres south of the abbey in the Fulda meadows. It was elevated to a subsidiary monastery under the Abbot Rabanus Maurus (around 780–856). The complex subsequently underwent several phases of conversion and expansion.

Monastic life at Johannesberg ended with the Thirty Years' War (1618–1648), and the former monastery became a provostry complex tasked with managing the extensive estate. The church was remodelled in the Baroque style as early as the end of the 17th century. *The rest of the complex mainly dates back to the tenure of Conrad von Mengersen (1677–1753, Provost from 1715), who redesigned it according to the plans by the prince-abbot court architect Andrea Gallasini (1681–1766) and added a new residential palace, the "Red Building".*

The gardens, which were also planned under Conrad von Mengersen and which extend eastwards towards Fulda, are divided into a large, upper terrace with two corner pavilions, fountains and sculptural ornaments as well as two further terraces.

KLOSTER KONRADSDORF, ORTENBERG

KONRADSDORF MONASTERY, ORTENBERG

Konrad, ein Lehensmann der Benediktinerabtei Fulda, errichtete im 8. Jahrhundert südwestlich von Ortenberg auf einer Anhöhe oberhalb der Nidder einen Herrenhof, der um das Jahr 1000 zu einer kleinen Burganlage ausgebaut und im ausgehenden 12. Jahrhundert in ein Kloster umgewandelt wurde. Klosterkirche und Propsteigebäude gehören heute zu den schönsten Bauten der Romanik in der Wetterau.

Kloster Konradsdorf
Am Kloster
63683 Ortenberg-Konradsdorf
www.schloesser-hessen.de/
de/kloster-konradsdorf

Das 1191 erstmals urkundlich erwähnte Kloster gehörte zum Prämonstratenserinnenorden und diente vor allem der Versorgung unverheirateter Frauen aus dem regionalen Adel. Durch Schenkungen erlangte es ansehnlichen Besitz. In seiner Blütezeit im 14. Jahrhundert lebten hier 64 Nonnen. Die Reformation setzte dem Klosterleben 1581 ein Ende.

Der schlicht gehaltene Kirchenbau, eine dreischiffige Pfeilerbasilika mit halbrunder Apsis, steht auf den Fundamenten einer kleineren fränkischen Saalkirche. Das nördliche Seitenschiff wurde im Dreißigjährigen Krieg (1618–1648) zerstört. Im Westen befand sich einst die Nonnenempore. Kunsthistorisch bedeutsam sind die Pfeilerkapitelle, die zum Teil mit Drachenköpfen verziert sind, sowie die Grabplatten der Familie von Breuberg aus dem Mittelalter.

Während die klösterlichen Wirtschaftsgebäude immer wieder erneuert wurden, hat sich aus der Romanik noch ein südlich an die Kirche angrenzender, zweigeschossiger Bau erhalten. Das einstige Wohnhaus des Propstes ist mit kostbaren Steinmetzarbeiten an den Fensterarkaden geschmückt und entsprach der repräsentativen Funktion dieses Würdenträgers, der die Geschäfte des Klosters nach außen vertrat.

In the 8th century, Conrad, a vassal of Fulda Benedictine Abbey, built a manor house on a hill to the south-west of Ortenberg. Sitting above the River Nidder, the manor house was converted into a small castle complex around 1000 and then into a monastery at the end of the 12th century. The monastery church and provostry building now represent some of the most beautiful Romanesque buildings in the Wetterau region.

◄ Romanisches Biforium in der Propstei
Romanic biforium window, former provost's residence

First mentioned in records in 1191, the monastery belonged to the Premonstratensian order. Its main purpose was to look after unmarried women of the local nobility. Gifts from them ensured the monastery accrued considerable property. 64 nuns lived at the monastery during its heyday in the 14th century, but monastery life came to an end with the Reformation.

The simple church building – a three-aisled pillared basilica with semicircular apse – stands on the foundations of a smaller Frankish aisleless church. The aisle on the north side was destroyed in the Thirty Years' War (1618–1648). The west side once housed a nuns' gallery. The pillar capitals, some of which are decorated with dragons' heads, are of artistic and historic importance, as are the memorial slabs of the von Breuberg family from the Middle Ages.

While the monastic agricultural buildings underwent several restorations, a two-storey Romanesque building adjoining the church on the south side has been preserved and was once the provost's residence. The building, whose window arcades are decorated with elaborate stonework, reflected the prestigious role performed by this dignitary, who represented the monastery in its dealings with the outside world.

KAISERPFALZ GELNHAUSEN

IMPERIAL PALACE OF GELNHAUSEN

Zusammen mit der Gründung der Stadt Gelnhausen ließ
der Stauferkaiser Friedrich I. Barbarossa (um 1122–1190)
um 1169/70 auf einer Kinziginsel eine Wasserburg anlegen. Die verkehrsgünstig an der Handelsstraße Via Regia
gelegene neue Pfalz diente fortan als Residenz – freilich
nur vorübergehend, denn um das riesige Reich zu sichern,
zogen Herrscher und Hofstaat permanent umher.

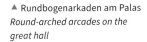 Rundbogenarkaden am Palas
Round-arched arcades on the great hall

Die Kaiserpfalz Gelnhausen war ein Machtzentrum des Heiligen Römischen Reiches Deutscher Nation. Im 12. Jahrhundert war sie Verwaltungssitz samt Wirtschaftshof, Stätte der Rechtsprechung, der Empfänge, Feste und Reichstage. Mit dem Niedergang der Staufer im 13. Jahrhundert verlor auch die Anlage ihre Bedeutung und vieles ging, beschleunigt durch die Nutzung als Steinbruch, verloren. Heute sind nur noch die Ruine des Palas, ein viereckiger Torturm und eine zweischiffige Torhalle mit Resten einer Kapelle sowie Teile der Umfassungsmauer erhalten.

Höhepunkt der Bauplastik ist die Ornamentik der Hoffassade des Palas mit Kleeblattbogenportal und gestaffelten Fensterarkaden.

Ein ehemaliges Burgmannenhaus im Westen der Kaiserpfalz dient heute als Museum. Zu den herausragenden Exponaten gehört ein kunstvoll gearbeitetes Kelchblockkapitell aus den Arkaden des Palas.

When founding the town of Gelnhausen, the emperor of the Staufen dynasty Friedrich I Barbarossa (around 1122–1190) had a moated castle built on an island in the Kinzig River around 1169/70. From then on the new palace, which was conveniently situated on the Via Regia trade route, served as a residence – albeit only on a temporary basis, because in order to secure the vast empire, rulers and their courts travelled around permanently.

◄ Kapitellplastik in der ehemaligen Pfalzkapelle
Capital sculptures in the former palatine chapel

Kaiserpfalz Gelnhausen
Burgstraße 14
63571 Gelnhausen
www.schloesser-hessen.de/
de/kaiserpfalz-gelnhausen

The Imperial Palace of Gelnhausen was a centre of power for the Holy Roman Empire of the German Nation. In the 12th century it was an administrative seat and included a farmyard and places for administering justice, for receptions and entertaining, and for holding parliaments. With the demise of the Staufen dynasty in the 13th century, the complex also declined in importance. Much was lost, a process hastened due to the complex being used as a quarry. Today, only the ruins of the palace, a square-shaped gate tower, a gate hall with two naves and the remains of a chapel remain, along with parts of the surrounding wall.

A highlight of the architectural sculpture is the ornamental decoration of the great hall's courtyard façade with its cloverleaf entrance portal and graduated window arcades.

A former knightly militia ("Burgmannen") house in the west of the imperial palace now serves as a museum. Notable exhibits include an artistically crafted bell-shaped block capital from the great hall's arcades.

KLOSTER UND KLOSTERGARTEN SELIGENSTADT

SELIGENSTADT ABBEY AND ABBEY GARDEN

Vom 9. bis ins 19. Jahrhundert lebten und arbeiteten Benediktinermönche in Kloster Seligenstadt. Hervorzuheben ist insbesondere der historische Apothekergarten des 18. Jahrhunderts, der einen wichtigen Part mönchischen Lebens dokumentiert: die Garten- und Heilkunst.

Kloster Seligenstadt
Ehemalige Benediktinerabtei
Klosterhof 2
63500 Seligenstadt
www.schloesser-hessen.de/
de/kloster-seligenstadt/

▶ Das „Engelsgärtchen"
im Klosterhof
*The "angel garden" in the
cloister courtyard*

▶ Heiliger Benedikt von Nursia,
Fresko im Sommerrefektorium
*Saint Benedict of Nursia, ceiling fresco
in the summer refectory*

◀ Das Sommerrefektorium mit
illusionistischem Freskenschmuck
*The summer refectory decorated
with illusionist frescoes*

Ein Besuch in Kloster Seligenstadt gewährt Einblick in das Leben nach der Ordensregel des heiligen Benedikt von Nursia (um 480–547). Dort heißt es: „Das Kloster soll, wenn möglich, so angelegt werden, dass sich alles Notwendige, nämlich Wasser, Mühle und Garten, innerhalb des Klosters befindet […]. So brauchen die Mönche nicht draußen herumlaufen, denn das ist für sie überhaupt nicht gut." Entsprechend dieser Regel funktionierte die 828 von Einhard (um 770–840), dem Berater und Biografen Karls des Großen (747/48–814), gegründete Benediktinerabtei bis zu ihrer Auflösung 1803 wie eine Stadt in der Stadt.

Eine erste Blüte erlebte das Kloster, damals unmittelbar den römisch-deutschen Herrschern unterstellt, im 11. Jahrhundert. Die zweite begann Ende des 17. Jahrhunderts, als die Anlage im Stil des Barock umgestaltet wurde – dieses barocke Ensemble hat bis heute überdauert.
Der Reichtum des Klosters im 18. Jahrhundert lässt sich bei einem Blick in die Prälatur ermessen: Im ersten Stock haben sich die Kaiserzimmer mit prächtigen Seidentapeten und monumentalen Gemälden in nahezu originalem Zustand erhalten.

◀ ▼ Der Garten mit dem Konvent-
gebäude und der Basilika
*The garden with the convent
building and the basilica*

▲ Apothekergarten
Pharmacy garden

Benedictine monks lived and worked at Seligenstadt Abbey from the 9th to the 19th centuries. Particular points of interest include the historical 18th-century pharmacy garden that documents garden design and the art of healing, an important part of monastic life.

A visit to Seligenstadt Abbey provides an insight into life under the monastic rule of Saint Benedict of Nursia (around 480–547). According to this monastic rule, "The monastery should, if possible, be so constructed that all necessities, such as water, mill and garden are contained within it [...]. Then there will be no need for the monks to roam outside, because this is not at all good for their souls". The Benedictine abbey, which was founded in 828 by Einhard (around 770–840), the advisor and biographer of Charlemagne (747/48–814), functioned according to this rule like a town within a town until its dissolution in 1803.

The abbey enjoyed a first heyday in the 11th century when it was directly subordinate to the Roman-German rulers. Its second heyday began at the end of the 17th century, when the complex was reconstructed in the Baroque style. This Baroque ensemble has survived until today.
The abbey's wealth in the 18th century can be gauged by a visit to the prelature. On the first floor, the imperial rooms have been preserved in almost pristine condition, with magnificent silk tapestries and huge paintings.

▶ Der Kreuzgang des Klosters Seligenstadt
The cloister at Seligenstadt Abbey

▼ Alkoven im Kaiserkabinett der Prälatur
Alcoves in the emperor's room of the prelature

EINHARDSBASILIKA, MICHELSTADT-STEINBACH

EINHARD'S BASILICA, MICHELSTADT-STEINBACH

Vor fast 1200 Jahren mitten in der Einsamkeit des Oden-
waldes errichtet und benannt nach ihrem Bauherrn
Einhard (um 770–840), einem der wichtigsten Vertrauten
Kaiser Karls des Großen (747/48–814), zählt die Basilika
heute zu den am besten erhaltenen karolingischen
Bauten Deutschlands.

Karls Nachfolger Ludwig der Fromme (778–840) schenkte Einhard das Gebiet rund um das heutige Seligenstadt sowie die sogenannte Mark Michelinstadt im Odenwald, wo sich Einhard zwischen 815 und 827 eine, wie er selbst schrieb, „prächtige Kirche von nicht unrühmlicher Art" erbauen ließ. Obwohl der dreischiffige Bau im Laufe der Zeit Eingriffe erfuhr, stammt die Substanz größtenteils aus der Karolingerzeit. Nach Einhards Tod 840 ging die Basilika in den Besitz des Klosters Lorsch über. Als die Landgrafschaft Hessen infolge der Reformation evangelisch wurde, kauften die Erbacher Grafen die Anlage. Jahrelang diente sie als Schuppen für Jagdgerät und als Holzlager. Die einfache hölzerne Dachkonstruktion aus dem 12. Jahrhundert ist bis heute erhalten.

827 ließ Einhard auf abenteuerlichen Wegen die aus einer römischen Katakombe geraubten Reliquien zweier frühchristlicher Märtyrer, der heiligen Marcellinus und Petrus, nach Steinbach holen. Bereits nach wenigen Monaten siedelte er die Reliquien nach Seligenstadt um, wo er eine noch größere Kirche errichtete.

Built almost 1200 years ago in the isolation of the Oden-wald Forest and named after its builder Einhard (around 770–840), who was one of the most important confidantes of Emperor Charlemagne (747/48–814), the Basilica is today one of the best-preserved Carolingian structures in Germany.

▶ Blick in das Mittelschiff zur Apsis
View towards the central nave in the direction of the apse

Charlemagne's successor Louis the Pious (778–840) gifted Einhard the area around what is today known as Seligenstadt as well as the mark of Michelinstadt in the Odenwald Forest, where Einhard, to quote his own words, had a "magnificent, not ignoble church" built between 815 and 827.

Although the three-aisled building suffered attacks over the years, most of its substance dates back to the Carolingian period. Following Einhard's death in 840 the Basilica passed into the hands of Lorsch Abbey. When the landgraviate of Hesse became Protestant following the Reformation, the complex was purchased by the Counts of Erbach. For years it served as a store for hunting equipment and wood. The simple wooden roof structure from the 12th century is still preserved today.

In 827, Einhard had the relics of two early Christian martyrs, Saint Marcellinus and Saint Peter, brought to Steinbach through dubious channels; these had previously been stolen from a Roman catacomb. After just a few months, he moved the relics to Seligenstadt, where he built an even bigger church.

▲ Grabplatte der 1512 verstorbenen Äbtissin Elisabeth Lochinger von Archshofen
Memorial slab of the abbess Elisabeth Lochinger von Archshofen, who died in 1512

Einhardsbasilika
Schlossstraße 17
64720 Michelstadt-Steinbach
www.schloesser-hessen.de/
de/einhardsbasilika

KLOSTER LORSCH, UNESCO-WELTERBE

LORSCH ABBEY, UNESCO WORLD HERITAGE SITE

Das um 764 gegründete Kloster Lorsch zählt zu den bedeutendsten Klosteranlagen des frühen Mittelalters und gehört seit 1991 zum UNESCO-Welterbe. Noch im 8. Jahrhundert wurde die Benediktinerabtei an Karl den Großen (747/48–814) übertragen, der sie zum Reichskloster machte und damit zum Agenten seiner Politik, die unter anderem Kirchen- und Bildungsreformen umfasste.

Kloster Lorsch
Museumszentrum Lorsch
Nibelungenstraße 35
64653 Lorsch
www.schloesser-hessen.de/
de/kloster-lorsch

◄ Blick auf die erhaltenen Teile
der Klosterkirche
*View towards the preserved parts
of the abbey church*

Unter dem fränkischen König und
Kaiser Karl dem Großen wurde Lorsch
reich und mächtig und erlangte insbesondere durch sein Skriptorium hohes
Ansehen. Noch zu Karls Zeiten entstand
hier das Lorscher Arzneibuch, die
älteste erhaltene medizinisch-pharma-
zeutische Handschrift aus nachantiker
Zeit.

Von der Klosteranlage haben sich heute
Reste der Basilika, die Klostermauer
und die berühmte Tor- oder Königshal-
le aus dem 9. Jahrhundert erhalten.
Letztere gilt als eines der wenigen
Zeugnisse karolingischer Architektur
unter römisch-antikem Einfluss in
Deutschland. Außerdem steht auf dem

Klosterareal eine Zehntscheune aus
dem 16. Jahrhundert, die heute der
Präsentation von Objekten aus über
200 Jahren Grabungsgeschichte dient.
Mit dem 2014 eröffneten Freilichtlabor
Lauresham bietet Lorsch zudem einen
Ort, an dem sich der Alltag der Menschen vor rund 1 200 Jahren erfahren
lässt – anhand des hier errichteten Ideal-
modells eines Herrenhofes aus der
Karolingerzeit mit Wohn- und Wirtschaftsgebäuden sowie dazugehörigen
Grünflächen. Dabei dient Lauresham
der Forschung: Experimentell befragen
und (re)konstruieren hier Wissen-
schaftler:innen die Vergangenheit und
ziehen daraus innovative Erkenntnisse.

Lorsch Abbey, founded in 764, is one of the most important abbey complexes from the early Middle Ages and has been a UNESCO World Heritage site since 1991. Back in the 8th century, the Benedictine abbey was transferred to Charlemagne (747/48–814). He made Lorsch an imperial abbey, and consequently an agent for his policies, which included reformation of the church and education.

▲ Die Lorscher Tor- oder Königshalle im Vordergrund, im Hintergrund Fragmente der Basilika des frühen 12. Jahrhunderts
The Lorsch Gatehouse, or King's Hall in the foreground, Fragments of the basilica dating back to the early 12th century in the background

▲ Die Bodengestaltung der Anlage macht die Dimensionen der verlorenen Bauten als Vertiefungen in der Rasenfläche erlebbar
The landform of the site makes it possible to perceive the dimensions of the lost buildings as hollows in the grass

◀ Bauskulptur mit dem Porträt eines Heiligen
Architectural sculpture with the portrait of a saint

◀ Sarkophag aus rotem Sandstein
Red sandstone sarcophagus

▲ Kräutergarten mit Pflanzen des Lorscher Arzneibuchs (um 795 n. Chr., Weltdokumentenerbe 2013)
Herb garden with plants from the Lorsch Pharmacopoeia (around 795 AD, Weltdokumentenerbe 2013)

Lorsch became rich and powerful under the Frankish king and emperor Charlemagne, acquiring fame for its scriptorium in particular. The Lorsch Pharmacopoeia was produced during the time of Charlemagne. It is the oldest preserved medical pharmaceutical manuscript from the post-antique epoch.

Of the abbey complex, remains of the basilica, the abbey walls and the famous Gatehouse Hall or King's Hall from the 9th century are still preserved today. The latter is one of the few examples of Carolingian architecture with Roman-antique influence in Germany. The abbey site also houses a 16th-century tithe barn, which is today used to exhibit items from over 200 years of excavation history.

Through the Lauresham Open-air Laboratory, opened in 2014, Lorsch also offers a place to experience the daily lives of people from around 1200 years ago. The laboratory is based on an idealised model of a Carolingian manor house with residential and farm buildings alongside green spaces. Lauresham is driving research in this field, with scientists conducting experiments to investigate and re-construct the past and drawing innovative findings from their work.

HANAU UND SEINE GRAFEN

HANAU AND ITS COUNTS

STAATSPARK HANAU-WILHELMSBAD

HANAU-WILHELMSBAD STATE PARK

Kuren und amüsieren – Wilhelmsbad, das sich Graf Wilhelm zu Hanau ab 1777 rund um eine Mineralquelle unweit Hanaus anlegen ließ, war bald ein auch von internationalem Publikum frequentiertes Kurbad. Heute sind die Gebäude des 18. Jahrhunderts und der sie umgebende Landschaftspark im englischen Stil fast vollständig erhalten und Zeugnis der Bäderkultur dieser Zeit.

Staatspark Hanau-Wilhelmsbad
Parkpromenade 7
63454 Hanau
www.schloesser-hessen.de/
de/hanau-wilhelmsbad

▲ Blick auf Brunnenhaus, Arkadenbau und Pavillon
*View of well house, arcade building
and pavilion*

◄ Die dem Mittelalter nachempfun-
dene Burgruine
*The castle ruins in the style of the
Middle Ages*

▼ Die Wilhelmsbader Promenade
The Wilhelmsbad Promenade

Wilhelmsbad verdankt seine Entste-
hung Wilhelm IX. (1743–1821) von
Hessen-Kassel, ab 1760 Graf zu Hanau.
Gemeinsam mit dem Baumeister und
Ingenieur Franz Ludwig Cancrin (1738–
1816) realisierte er die Anlage im spät-
barocken Stil.

Die Kurgebäude liegen an einer Promenade aufgereiht inmitten eines
Landschaftsparks. Heute noch lassen
sich dort entlang gewundener Pfade
Aussichtspunkte und Zierbauten entdecken, darunter eine Grotte, eine Ein-
siedelei und der sogenannte Schne-
ckenberg. Der Unterhaltung dienten
außerdem das Comoedienhaus sowie
ein Karussell, das heute als ältestes

feststehendes der Welt gilt und bis in
die Gegenwart hinein fährt. Bemer-
kenswert ist außerdem des Grafen per-
sönliches Refugium, eine künstliche
Ruine: Ihre Außenfassaden kontrastie-
ren mit einer Reihe kostbar ausgestat-
teter Innenräume.

1785 wurde Wilhelm Landgraf von Hessen-Kassel und verließ Hanau. Zweifel
an der Heilkraft der Quelle – sie sollte
Gebrechen wie „Eingeweidewürmer"
und „Bleichsucht" vertreiben – sorgten
für den Niedergang des Bäderbetriebs,
aber auch dafür, dass die Anlage in
ihrem Erscheinungsbild nahezu unverändert erhalten blieb.

Taking a cure and having fun – the spa resort of Wilhelms-bad, which the Count William of Hanau had built around a mineral spring not far from Hanau from 1777, was soon also frequented by international visitors. Today, the 18th century buildings and the English landscape garden in which they sit are preserved almost in their entirety, bearing testimony to the spa culture of the time.

▲ Das Karussell von Wilhelmsbad
The Wilhelmsbad carousel

◄ Unterkonstruktion des Karussells
Substructure of the carousel

▲ Kabinette im Inneren
der Burgruine
*Small rooms in the interior
of the ruined castle*

Wilhelmsbad owes its existence to Wilhelm IX (1743–1821) of Hesse-Kassel, Count of Hanau from 1760. He worked with the builder and engineer Franz Ludwig Cancrin (1738–1816) to build the complex in late Baroque style.

The spa buildings are built along a promenade in the middle of a landscape park. Winding paths through the park reveal viewpoints and ornamental structures including a grotto, a hermitage, and a hill built to resemble a snail's shell. Entertainment was also provided by the Comoedienhaus theatre and by a carousel, which is still in working order today and is the

world's oldest fixed carousel. Another highlight is an artificial ruin that served as the Count's own personal place of refuge. Its external façades are in contrast to a series of splendidly furnished inner rooms.

In 1785, Wilhelm became Landgrave of Hesse-Kassel and left Hanau. Doubts about the salutary effects of the waters – which were said to drive away ailments such as "intestinal worms" and "anaemia" – prompted the decline of the spa but also ensured that the complex's appearance remained preserved almost in its entirety.

SCHLOSS STEINAU

STEINAU PALACE

Als eines der bedeutendsten Renaissanceschlösser in Hessen stellt Schloss Steinau eine Synthese zwischen Festungsarchitektur und repräsentativem Schlossbau dar. Hinter dem wehrhaften Äußeren überrascht es mit Resten feinster Renaissanceausstattung und einer Fülle lokalhistorischer Besonderheiten. Nicht zuletzt erinnert die 2015 eröffnete Grimm-Ausstellung daran, dass die beiden Brüder ihre Kindheit in Steinau an der Straße verbrachten.

Schloss Steinau a. d. Straße
36396 Steinau a. d. Straße
www.schloesser-hessen.de/
de/schloss-steinau

▶ Türmerstube auf dem Bergfried
Watchman's room at the castle's keep

▶ Blick aus dem nördlichen Tor
in den Zwinger
*View from the northern castle gate
to the kennel*

Schloss Steinau liegt im Kinzigtal an der Via Regia, der einst wichtigen Handelsstraße zwischen Frankfurt und Leipzig. Im 12. Jahrhundert gegründet und immer wieder erweitert, war der Umbau zur bastionierten fünfeckigen Renaissancefestung unter den Grafen von Hanau-Münzenberg im frühen 16. Jahrhundert prägend für das heutige Erscheinungsbild der Anlage. Damals ließen die Grafen auch die Innenräume prachtvoll ausstatten. Qualitätsvolle Wandmalereien mit Renaissance-Ornamenten und antikisierenden Porträtmedaillons zierten die Säle und Appartements. Die Ausmaße der An-lage und die aufwendige Ausstattung sprechen dafür, dass Schloss Steinau ursprünglich als Nebenresidenz der Grafen von Hanau-Münzenberg dienen sollte. Als ein Teil der Hanauer Territorien 1736 an die Landgrafschaft Hessen-Kassel fiel, verlor das Schloss seine einstige Bedeutung und blieb in der Folgezeit von Umbauten weitgehend verschont. Dank ihres außergewöhnlich guten Erhaltungszustands vermittelt die Anlage einen authentischen Eindruck vom Aussehen eines befestigten Schlossbaus an der Epochenschwelle zwischen Mittelalter und Neuzeit.

One of the most important Renaissance palaces in Hesse, Steinau Palace combines fortified architecture with elegant palace construction. Behind its defensive exterior, the palace surprises visitors with remnants of finest Renaissance characteristics and a wealth of special local historic features. The Brothers Grimm Exhibition, opened in 2015, commemorates the fact that the famous brothers spent their childhood in Steinau an der Straße.

▼ Blick in die Hofstube
View of the courtroom

Steinau Palace is situated in the Kinzig Valley on the Via Regia, once an important trade route between Frankfurt and Leipzig. Founded in the 12th century and extended multiple times, the castle's remodelling into a bastioned pentagonal Renaissance fortification under the Counts of Hanau-Münzenberg in the early 16th century had a formative influence on its current appearance.

The Counts also ensured the internal spaces were furnished in magnificent style. The rooms and apartments were decorated with quality wall paintings that feature Renaissance ornaments and antique-style portrait medallions. The scale of the complex and its lavish décor indicate that Steinau Palace was originally intended as a secondary residence for the Counts of Hanau Münzenberg.

When part of the Hanau territories fell to the landgraviate of Hesse-Kassel in 1736, the palace lost its former importance and was subsequently largely spared subsequent remodelling. Thanks to its exceptionally well-preserved state, the complex conveys an authentic impression of a fortified palace structure at the threshold between the Middle Ages and the modern era.

BURG- UND SCHLOSSRUINE SCHWARZENFELS

SCHWARZENFELS CASTLE AND PALACE RUINS

Burg Schwarzenfels liegt hoch über dem Sinntal am Westhang des Hopfenberges. Ihren Namen verdankt sie wohl dem schwarzen Basalt, aus dem diese Anhöhe besteht. Von Weitem schon zeigen sich das repräsentative ehemalige Marstallgebäude und die mittelalterliche Burgruine mit mächtigem Bergfried.

Es war wohl der Stammvater der Herren von Hanau, Reinhard I. (um 1225–1281), der die 1280 erstmals urkundlich erwähnte Burg Schwarzenfels als strategischen Stützpunkt errichtete. 1333 erhielten die Herren von Hanau das Gebiet um Schwarzenfels als Reichslehen.

Größere Veränderungen der Anlage erfolgten, als die Witwe des Grafen Philipp III. von Hanau-Münzenberg (1526–1561), Helene von Pfalz-Simmern (1532–1579), die Burg bezog. Sie passte ihr neues Domizil ihren Ansprüchen an und ließ unter anderem eine Badestube einrichten. Bereits 1551 hatte ihr Ehemann den Marstall

errichten lassen. Albrecht von Hanau-Münzenberg (1579–1635) nutzte Schwarzenfels als Residenz und nahm weitere Umbauten vor, von denen ein prachtvolles Portal mit Brunnenvorbau erhalten geblieben ist.

Im Dreißigjährigen Krieg (1618–1648) wurde die Burg zerstört und nur der Marstall als Verwaltungsgebäude weiter genutzt. Bis heute ist dieses Gebäude das Zentrum der Anlage. Aber auch die Burgruine bietet neue Attraktionen: den Schwarzenfelser Skywalk, eine gläserne Aussichtsplattform am Bergfried, die über das Mauerwerk hinausragt und herrliche Ausblicke erlaubt.

Burg- und Schlossruine
Schwarzenfels
Schloßgasse 24
36391 Sinntal, Schwarzenfels
www.schloesser-hessen.de/
de/burgruine-schwarzenfels

Schwarzenfels Castle sits high above the Sinn Valley on the western slope of the Hopfenberg. It probably owes its name to the black basalt which forms this hill. The representative former stables building and the ruined medieval castle with its mighty keep can be seen from afar.

It was probably the founding father of the Lords of Hanau, Reinhard I (around 1225–1281), who built Schwarzenfels Castle, first mentioned in records in 1280, as a strategic base. In 1333, the Lords of Hanau received the area around Schwarzenfels as an imperial fiefdom.

Major changes to the complex followed, when Helene of Pfalz-Simmern (1532–1579), widow of Count Philipp III of Hanau-Münzenberg (1526–1561), moved into the castle. She adapted her new domicile to suit her requirements and had a bath house built, among other things. Her husband had already had the stables built back in 1551. Finally, Albrecht of Hanau-Münzenberg (1579–1635) used Schwarzenfels as a residence and undertook further modifications, of which a splendid portal with fountain in front of it has been preserved.

The castle was destroyed during the Thirty Years' War (1618–48). After this, only the stables building was still used, as an administrative building. Today, this building still forms the centre of the complex. However, even the castle ruins offer new attractions in the form of the Schwarzenfels Skywalk, a glass viewing platform on the keep that extends beyond the brickwork to offer amazing views.

DARMSTADT UND BERGSTRASSE

DARMSTADT AND THE MOUNTAIN ROAD

PRINZ-GEORG-GARTEN, DARMSTADT

PRINCE GEORGE GARDEN, DARMSTADT

Eine Oase der Ruhe mitten in der Stadt: Heute ist der
Prinz-Georg-Garten für jedermann zugänglich, einst
war er einem Prinzen vorbehalten. Landgraf Ludwig VIII.
von Hessen-Darmstadt (1691–1768) schenkte den Garten
1764 seinem zweitgeborenen Sohn Georg Wilhelm
(1722–1782), der ihn fortan als Refugium nutzte.

Prinz-Georg-Garten
Schlossgartenstraße 6b
64289 Darmstadt
www.schloesser-hessen.de/
de/prinz-georg-garten

▲ Barocke Sonnenuhr
Baroque sundial

Die geometrisch-formale Ordnung des Prinz-Georg-Gartens mit seinen Rasenflächen, Fontänen, Bosketten und Sonnenuhren lässt den Einfluss französischer Gärten erkennen. Die Anlage entstand aus der Zusammenlegung zweier Gärten, was bis heute am Grundriss ablesbar ist. Den einen Teil hatte bereits Ludwigs Vater angelegt und dort um 1710 ein kleines barockes Palais errichten lassen, das heutige Prinz-Georg-Palais. Außerdem kaufte Ludwig das unmittelbar angrenzende Grundstück des Generalleutnants Rudolf von Pretlack (1668–1737) hinzu, zu dem ein mit Orangenbäumchen, Ranken und Girlanden bemaltes Gartenhaus gehörte.

Auf besondere Art verbunden wurden hier Zier- und Nutzgarten: In den von Buchshecken eingefassten Beeten wechselten sich Blumen, Obstgehölze, Kräuter und Gemüse ab. Da im 20. Jahrhundert eine umfassende Rekonstruktion der historischen Bepflanzung stattfand, ist dies noch immer nachvollziehbar.

Im Pretlack'schen Gartenhaus befindet sich heute eine öffentliche Bibliothek, während das Prinz-Georg-Palais seit 1908 die Großherzoglich-Hessische-Porzellansammlung beherbergt.

An oasis of calm in the heart of the city – once the reserve of a prince, the Prince George Garden is today open to everyone. In 1764, Landgrave Ludwig VIII of Hesse-Darmstadt (1691–1768) gifted the garden to his second and favourite son, Georg Wilhelm (1722–1782), who from then on used it as an intimate refuge.

▶ Treillage mit Sonnenmaske
Trellis with sun mask

▼ Barocke Sonnenuhr und Prinz-Georg-Palais
Baroque sundial and Prince George House

The formal, geometric layout with lawned areas, fountains, thickets and sundials reveals the influence of French gardens on the design of the Prince George Garden. The complex was formed by combining two gardens, a fact which is still visible today from the garden's layout. Ludwig's father had already created one part and had a small Baroque palace (now known as Prince George Palace) constructed there around 1710. Ludwig also purchased the adjoining plot belonging to Lieutenant General Rudolf von Pretlack (1668–1737), which included a pretty summer house painted with small orange trees, vines and garlands.

The site cleverly combined ornamental and kitchen gardens. Surrounded by boxwood hedges, beds contained flowers, fruit trees, herbs and vegetables. Extensive restoration of the historical planting in the 20th century has ensured these can still be seen today.

The Pretlack'sches summer house now houses a public library, while the Prince George Palace has housed the Grand Ducal-Hessian Porcelain Collection since 1908.

▶ Pretlack'sches Gartenhaus
Summer house of Rudolf von Pretlack

FÜRSTENGRUFT DARMSTADT

THE FÜRSTENGRUFT PRINCELY CRYPT DARMSTADT

Unter dem Chor der evangelischen Stadtkirche in Darmstadt liegt die Ruhestätte der Landgrafen von Hessen-Darmstadt. Noch im 16. Jahrhundert angelegt, ließ Landgraf Ludwig V. (1577–1626) sie mit aufwendigen Stuckarbeiten ausstatten sowie mit einem Epitaph, das ihn als Stifter der „Hohen Schule in Gießen" (heute: Justus-Liebig-Universität) und Hüter des lutherischen Glaubens inszeniert.

Fürstengruft
An der Stadtkirche 1
64283 Darmstadt
www.schloesser-hessen.de/
de/fuerstengruft-darmstadt

Georg I. (1547–1596) von Hessen-Darmstadt begann wahrscheinlich schon um 1576 mit der Anlage der Fürstengruft unter dem Chor der Stadtkirche. Die Gruft bestand zunächst aus einem länglichen Raum mit schmucklosem Tonnengewölbe, wurde aber schon einige Jahre später um ein zweites Gewölbe erweitert.

Georgs Nachfolger Landgraf Ludwig V. ließ 1615 beide Kammern mit farbigem und vergoldetem Stuck ausschmücken. Das Bildprogramm erzählt die christliche Heilsgeschichte mit Grablegung, Auferstehung und Himmelfahrt Christi sowie dem Jüngsten Gericht, wobei sich der Landgraf in dieser Szene unterhalb des richtenden Christus zusammen mit seinem Vater und seiner Ehefrau selbst verewigen ließ. Betrachter:innen werden so an ihre eigene Sterblichkeit erinnert (Memento mori), aber auch an die Hoffnung auf Erlösung im christlichen Glauben.

Heute befinden sich in der Fürstengruft 17 Särge, meistenteils von Landgrafen und Landgräfinnen. Eine Besonderheit sind die beiden metallenen Kapseln, die von der Decke des vorderen Gewölbes hängen und die Herzen der Prinzen Georg (1669–1705) und Philipp (1671–1736) von Hessen-Darmstadt enthalten, die fern der Heimat verstarben.

146

The resting place of the landgraves of Hesse-Darmstadt lies beneath the chancel of the Protestant City Church in Darmstadt. Created back in the 16th century, Landgrave Ludwig V (1577–1626) had it decorated with elaborate stucco works and an epitaph that presents him as benefactor of the "College in Gießen" (today: Justus-Liebig University Giessen) and guardian of the Lutheran faith.

George I (1547–1596) of Hesse-Darmstadt probably began to create the princely crypt below the city church's chancel as early as around 1576. Although the crypt initially consisted of an elongated room with one plain barrel vault, a second vault was added just a few years later.

In 1615, George's successor, Landgrave Ludwig V, had both chambers decorated with coloured and gilded stucco ornaments. The series of images recounts the story of Christian salvation with Christ's entombment, resurrection and ascension. It also depicts the Last Judgement in a scene where the landgrave, together with his father and his wife, themselves become immortalised below Christ as judge. Observers are thus reminded of their own mortality (memento mori), but also of the hope of salvation in the Christian faith. Today, the Princely Crypt holds 17 caskets, mainly of landgraves and landgravines. Of note are the two metal capsules which hang from the ceiling of the front vault, and which contain the hearts of Prince George (1669–1705) and Prince Philipp (1671–1736) of Hesse-Darmstadt, who died far from their home.

BURGRUINE FRANKEN-STEIN, MÜHLTAL

FRANKENSTEIN CASTLE RUINS, MÜHLTAL

Frankenstein – schon der Name erzeugt Gruseln. Zuerst hat die Engländerin Mary Shelley (1797–1851) die Geschichte des künstlichen Menschen und seines Schöpfers Viktor Frankenstein erzählt. Trotz anders lautender Vermutungen war Shelley aber wohl nie auf der Burg, die auch im Roman keine Rolle spielt. Dennoch finden hier alljährlich zu Halloween Schauerspektakel statt.

The very name "Frankenstein" is enough to make the flesh creep. The English author Mary Shelley (1793–1851) first told the story of the artificial human and his creator Viktor Frankenstein. However, contrary to suppositions, Shelley probably never visited the castle, which also plays no role in the novel. Nevertheless, a spooky festival takes place here every year around Halloween.

Die Burg liegt wenige Kilometer südlich von Darmstadt im Odenwald. 1252 wird sie erstmals in Zusammenhang mit ihrem vermutlichen Erbauer, Konrad Reiz von Breuberg (?–1264), erwähnt, der sich später von Frankenstein nannte.

Aus dem 13. Jahrhundert sind die südlichen Teile der Kernburg mit Turm und Palas erhalten, an denen noch heute die Enge der Anlage ablesbar ist. Um 1400 wurde die Frankenstein um die nördlich gelegene Vorburg mit Wirtschaftsgebäuden und Gesindewohnungen erweitert. Nach Jahren der Auseinandersetzungen mit den protestantischen Landgrafen von Hessen-Darmstadt – die Frankensteiner hielten am katholischen Glauben fest – verkaufte die Familie 1662 die Burg an Hessen-Darmstadt. In der Folge verfiel die Anlage.

Bereits Anfang des 19. Jahrhunderts begann die touristische Entdeckung der Burgruine und damit ihre Pflege. Besonders attraktiv war und ist die wunderbare Lage mitten im Wald mit herrlicher Aussicht auf die Rheinebene. Die Tradition der Schauerspektakel auf der Burg haben übrigens in der Region stationierte US-Soldaten bereits in den 1970er-Jahren begründet.

Burgruine Frankenstein
64367 Mühltal
www.schloesser-hessen.de/
de/burg-frankenstein

The castle lies a few kilometres south of Darmstadt in the Odenwald Forest. It was first mentioned in 1252 together with its probable builder, Konrad Reiz von Breuberg (?–1264), who later changed his name to von Frankenstein.

The southern sections of the central part of the castle including the tower and great hall dating back to the 13th century are still preserved and reveal the narrowness of the complex. Around 1400, Frankenstein Castle was extended to add the northern outer bailey with farm buildings and servants' quarters. After years of conflict with the Protestant landgraves

of Hesse-Darmstadt, the Frankensteins, who remained true to the Catholic faith, sold the castle to Hesse-Darmstadt in 1662. The complex subsequently fell into disrepair.

Upkeep of the castle recommenced as tourists discovered the castle ruins at the start of the 19th century. The castle's delightful setting in the middle of the forest with its amazing view of the Rhine Valley was and still is a particularly striking feature. Interestingly, the tradition of the Halloween festival at the castle was started in the 1970s by US airmen stationed in the region.

STAATSPARK FÜRSTENLAGER, BENSHEIM-AUERBACH

FÜRSTENLAGER STATE PARK, BENSHEIM-AUERBACH

Die Entwicklung hin zu einem prächtigen Kurbad blieb dem Fürstenlager verwehrt. Dafür entdeckten die Landgrafen von Hessen-Darmstadt dieses als Sommerresidenz. Verborgen in einem Seitental an der Bergstraße am Rande des Odenwaldes, beeindruckt das Fürstenlager bis heute mit einer dorfartigen Anlage und einem etwa 46 Hektar großen, landschaftlich gestalteten Park.

Staatspark Fürstenlager
64625 Bensheim-Auerbach
www.schloesser-
hessen.de/de/fuerstenlager

Im Jahr 1739 wurden in Auerbach drei nahe beieinanderliegende Mineralquellen gefunden. Ein kontinuierlicher Kurbetrieb etablierte sich, als 1766 eine Einfassung aus Stein um die Quellen errichtet wurde. Schließlich traf 1767 Landgraf Ludwig VIII. von Hessen-Darmstadt (1691–1768) zur Kur ein. Die ersten dauerhaften Gebäude, zwei Pavillons, wurden errichtet.

Unter Landgraf Ludwig X. (1753–1830) und seiner Frau Luise (1761–1829) erlebte das Fürstenlager ab 1783 eine neue Blüte als Sommerresidenz. Zwischen 1790 und 1795 entstand um den zentralen Gesundbrunnen die das Fürstenlager bis heute prägende, dorfartige Anlage. Die einzelnen Gebäude, darunter Fremden- und Kavaliersbau, Prinzen- und Damenbau, Wache und Remisen sind noch immer nahezu unverändert erhalten.

Mit dem Ausbau der Gebäude wurde Ende des 18. Jahrhunderts auch ein nach den Prinzipien des englischen Landschaftsgartens gestalteter Park angelegt. Hofgärtner Carl Ludwig Geiger konnte durch seine umsichtige Arbeit den ländlichen Charakter des Areals bewahren. Mit Pappeln bepflanzte Alleen führen heute noch Besucher:innen zu auf den Anhöhen liegenden Parkarchitekturen, Schmuck- und Aussichtsplätzen.

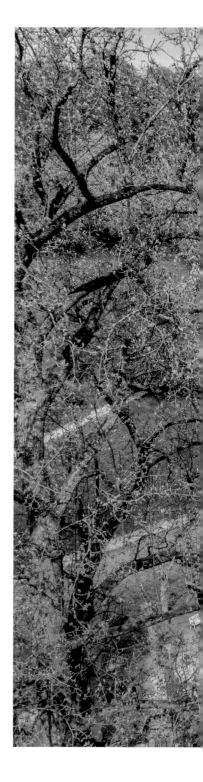

Although the Fürstenlager State Park failed to develop into a splendid spa resort, the landgraves of Hesse-Darmstadt discovered it as a summer residence. Hidden in a side valley along the mountain road on the edge of the Odenwald Forest, the Fürstenlager State Park is still an impressive sight today with a village-like structure and a landscaped park extending to around 46 hectares.

In 1739, three mineral springs were discovered adjacent to each other in Auerbach. A steady spa business developed after rocks were used to enclose the springs in 1766. Then in 1767, Landgrave Louis VIII of Hesse-Darmstadt (1691–1768) visited Auerbach for a cure. The first permanent buildings consisting of two pavilions were built.

From 1783, the Fürstenlager State Park enjoyed a revival as a summer residence under Landgrave Louis X (1753–1830) and his wife Louise (1761–1829). The village-like structure that still gives the Fürstenlager State Park its characteristic appearance was built around the central health-giving springs between 1790 and 1795. The individual buildings, including the Fremden- und Kavaliersbau (guests' building and cavalry building), the Prinzen- und Damenbau (princes' and women's building), the Wache (guardhouse) and the Remisen (outbuildings) have been preserved almost in their entirety.

As the buildings were expanded at the end of the 18th century, a park was also created based on the principles of English landscape garden design. Court gardener Carl Ludwig Geiger's careful approach ensured the area was able to preserve its rural character. Today, avenues lined with poplar trees still lead visitors to the park buildings, ornamental areas and viewing points sited on the hills.

SCHLOSS AUERBACH
AUERBACH PALACE

Die im 13. Jahrhundert angelegte und im 14. Jahrhundert umfassend erneuerte Burganlage liegt oberhalb von Bensheim-Auerbach auf einem der westlichsten Ausläufer des Odenwaldes. Das eigentliche Wahrzeichen der Burganlage ist botanischer Natur: Eine über 300 Jahre alte Kiefer, die sich mitten auf dem Wehrgang verwurzelt hat.

Schloss Auerbach
64625 Auerbach
www.schloesser-hessen.de/
de/schloss-auerbach

▼ Fenster in der Kapelle
am Palas
*Window in the chapel
of the Palas*

Im 13. Jahrhundert kontrollierten die Grafen von Katzenelnbogen die Bergstraße, einen schon in römischer Zeit genutzten Handelsweg. Zolleinnahmen am Mittelrhein hatten die Familie reich und mächtig gemacht. Ihre Herrschaft sicherten sie, indem sie zahlreiche Burgen zwischen Taunus und Odenwald errichteten – so auch das Auerbacher Schloss.

Die Kernburg mit dreieckigem Hof umfassen zwei Ringmauern mit einem schmalen inneren Zwinger (Jungfernzwinger) sowie einem äußeren Zwinger, die jeweils der Verteidigung dienten: Überwanden Angreifer die Burgmauer, so konnten sie im Zwinger eingekesselt werden. Während der Bergfried bereits 1356 bei einem Erdbeben einstürzte, stehen die beiden runden Ecktürme bis heute und prägen die Silhouette des Schlosses. Von besonderem Interesse ist auch der Palas: Die dreistöckige Wohnburg der Grafen aus dem 14. Jahrhundert steht noch immer – fast in voller Höhe, allerdings ohne Dach und Zwischenwände.

1674 zerstört, blieb das Auerbacher Schloss seitdem Ruine.

▲ Blick vom Wehrgang
in den Palas
*View from the walk-walk
into the palace*

Built in the 13th century and extensively renovated in the 14th century, the castle complex is situated above Bensheim-Auerbach on one of the western foothills of the Odenwald Forest. The real landmark of the castle complex is botanic in nature – a pine tree that is over 300 years old and has become rooted in the middle of the wall-walk.

In the 13th century, the counts of Katzenelnbogen controlled the Bergstraße, a trade route through the hills of the Odenwald Forest that was used as early as Roman times. Customs revenues on the Middle Rhine had made the family rich and powerful. They secured their rule by building numerous castles between the Taunus hills and the Odenwald Forest – including Auerbach Palace.

The central part of the castle with its triangular courtyard is surrounded by two curtain walls with a narrow internal ward (Jungfernzwinger, or Maiden's Ward) and an outer ward, each of which were used for defence: attackers who managed to surmount the curtain wall could be contained within the ward. Although the keep collapsed as early as 1356 during an earthquake, the two round corner towers are still standing today and define the palace's silhouette. The great hall is another highlight: the Counts' residential castle of the 14th century comprises three floors and still stands at almost its full height today, albeit minus its roof and dividing walls.

Auerbach Palace has remained a ruin since it was destroyed in 1674.

AM RHEIN

ON THE
RIVER RHINE

SCHLOSSPARK BIEBRICH, WIESBADEN

BIEBRICH PALACE PARK, WIESBADEN

Der Schlosspark in Wiesbaden-Biebrich ist das letzte Werk des bedeutenden Gartenkünstlers Friedrich Ludwig von Sckell (1750–1823) und eine Perle der Gartenkunst. Die rechteckige Parkanlage erstreckt sich über 1200 Meter hinter der am Ufer des Rheins gelegenen dreiflügeligen Schlossanlage. Einen besonderen Höhepunkt bildet die Mosburg, die als Belvedere errichtet wurde.

Der 67-jährige erfahrene Hofgartenintendant Sckell schuf 1817 in dem langgestreckten, flachen Gelände einen einzigartigen englischen Landschaftsraum mit einem mittig gelegenen Wiesental, das beidseitig von unregelmäßigen Gehölzriegeln eingefasst wird. Zugute kamen ihm hierbei die geometrische Wegeführung mit Alleen aus der unter Fürst Friedrich August von Nassau-Usingen (1738–1816) von Maximilian von Welsch (1671–1745) um 1721 entworfenen barocken Gartenanlage. Auch den vorhandenen Küchen- und Kräutergarten integrierte er in die Planungen.

Sckells Nachfolge übernahm ab 1846 der bekannte Gartenkünstler Carl Friedrich Thelemann (1811–1889). Unter ihm entstanden ab 1850 die Biebricher Gewächshäuser, die bald Pflanzen aus aller Welt beherbergten. Allerdings nur kurz, denn bereits 1869 wurden die 20 000 Pflanzen mitsamt der Gewächshäuser nach Frankfurt überführt – die neu gegründete Palmengartengesellschaft hatte sie erworben.

Heute finden sich in Biebrich noch eine Orangerie und ein Ananashaus. Mit Springbrunnen, Mosburgweiher, Bachlauf und dem Rheinstrom entführt der Park Besucher:innen an einen einzigartigen Ort.

▼ Schloss Biebrich mit dem Fontänenbecken
Biebrich Palace with fountain pool

▶ Die Mosburg
The Mosburg

Representing the final work of renowned landscape architect Friedrich Ludwig von Sckell (1750–1823), the palace park in the borough of Biebrich in Wiesbaden is a gem of garden design. The rectangular park extends to over 1,200 metres behind the three-wing castle complex on the banks of the Rhine. The Mosburg, which was built as a Belvedere, is a particular highlight.

Schlosspark Biebrich
65203 Wiesbaden
www.schloesser-hessen.de/
de/schlosspark-biebrich

In 1817 at the age of 67, the experienced court garden designer Sckell created a unique English garden landscape space on the elongated, flat terrain. His design included a central meadow valley bordered on both sides by irregularly placed clusters of trees. He was able to use the geometric pathways and avenues from the Baroque gardens designed in around 1721 by Maximilian von Welsch (1671–1745) under Prince Friedrich August of Nassau-Usingen (1738–1816). He also integrated the existing kitchen and herb garden into his plans.

The renowned landscape architect Carl Friedrich Thelemann (1811–1889) took over as Sckell's successor in 1846 and started to install glasshouses at Biebrich from 1850. These soon gave shelter to plants from around the world – albeit only for a short period, as the 20,000 plants together with the glasshouses were moved to Frankfurt in 1869 when they were acquired by the newly established Palm Garden Company.

Today, Biebrich still has an orangery and a pineapple house. With its water fountains, Mosburg pond, stream and section of the Rhine, the park offers a unique place for visitors to explore.

161

BRENTANO-HAUS, OESTRICH-WINKEL

BRENTANO HOUSE, OESTRICH-WINKEL

Das zweistöckige Gebäude mit Mansarddach nebst einem bis zum Rhein reichenden Grundstück kam 1806 in Besitz der Familie Brentano, die es als Sommersitz nutzte. Über 200 Jahre blieb das 1751 erbaute Anwesen im Eigentum der Nachkommen, bis es das Land Hessen übernahm. Das gut erhaltene Landgut gibt Einblicke in die Lebenswelt einer bürgerlichen Familie zur Zeit der Romantik.

Brentano-Haus
Am Lindenplatz 2
65375 Oestrich-Winkel
www.schloesser-hessen.de/
de/brentano-haus

▲ Der Innenhof des Landguts
The estate's inner courtyard

◀ Der große Salon in der Beletage
The Great Parlour on the first floor

Vor allem Franz Brentano (1765–1844) nutzte das schöne Landgut in Oestrich-Winkel als geselligen Treffpunkt. Zu den prominenten Besuchenden der Familie zählte 1814 Johann Wolfgang von Goethe (1749–1832). In seinem später veröffentlichten Tagebuch dankte er der Familie Brentano, die ihm „an den Ufern des Rheins, auf ihrem Landgute zu Winkel viele glückliche Stunden" bereitet habe. Die Räume, die er bewohnte, beließ man in ihrem Zustand, sodass sie noch heute zu besichtigen sind.

Die jüngeren Geschwister von Franz, Clemens (1778–1842) und insbesondere Bettina (verheiratete von Arnim; 1785–1859), stilisierten das Haus dort später zu einem Ort des romantischen Freundschaftskultes. So schrieb die Dichterin, sie hätten „die Nächte am Rhein verschwärmt" und seien „auf dem prächtigen Rheinspiegel in Mondnächten" dahingeglitten.

▲ Der Rote Salon
The Red Parlour

In 1806, the two-storey building with mansard roof and land extending to the River Rhine came into the ownership of the Brentano family, who used it as a summer residence. The manor house, which had been built in 1751, remained in the family for over 200 years, when it was taken over by the State of Hesse. The well-preserved estate gives an insight into the lifestyle of a bourgeois family in the Romantic period.

▲ Goethes Arbeitszimmer
Goethe's study

*Franz Brentano (1765–1844) in particu-
lar used the beautiful estate in Oestrich-
Winkel as a place for social gatherings.
The list of the family's prominent visitors
included Johann Wolfgang von Goethe
(1749–1832) in 1814. In his diary, which
was published later, he thanked the
Brentano family, with whom he had spent
"many happy hours on the banks of the
Rhine at their estate in Winkel". The rooms
in which he stayed were left in their original condition in his honour and can still
be viewed today.*

*Franz's younger siblings, Clemens (1778–
1842) and in particular Bettina (whose
married name was von Arnim; 1785–1859),
later styled the house there as a place of
Romantic friendship cult.
A noted poet, von Armin wrote that they
spent "nights of revelry along the Rhine"
and "glided upon the splendid mirror of
the Rhine by moonlight".*

ZEPPELINDENKMAL, TREBUR-GEINSHEIM

ZEPPELIN MONUMENT, TREBUR-GEINSHEIM

Graf Ferdinand von Zeppelin (1838–1917) musste auf einem Dauerflug von Konstanz nach Mainz bei Geinsheim am Rhein am 4. August 1908 wegen eines Motorendefekts notlanden. Grund genug, hier bereits ein Jahr später ein Denkmal zu errichten, das an das Ereignis erinnert, und damit auch an die große Begeisterung für die „Giganten der Lüfte" in der Kaiserzeit.

▼ Die Inschrift lautet: Hier landete mit seinem Luftschiff Graf Zeppelin auf seiner ersten Dauerfahrt am 4. August 1918
The inscription reads: On 4 August 1918, Count Zeppelin landed here with his airship during his first long-distance flight.

Im Jahr 1900 war dem Grafen Ferdinand von Zeppelin (1838–1917) mit seinem durch ein Metallgerüst stabilisierten Starrluftschiff ein Durchbruch gelungen: Die Technologie revolutionierte den zivilen und militärischen Luftverkehr. Zeppeline flogen damals höher und weiter als Propellerflugzeuge und trugen schwerere Lasten.

Ein Unglücksfall ereignete sich jedoch im südhessischen Geinsheim: Auf seinem ersten Langstreckenflug am 4. August 1908 musste der Graf sein LZ-4-Modell notlanden. Zwar erreichte er noch am selben Abend Mainz, musste aber am Folgetag auf dem Rückflug nach Konstanz erneut einen unfreiwilligen Zwischenhalt einlegen. Dort riss sich das Schiff aus der Verankerung und ging schließlich in Flammen auf.

Schon ein Jahr später wurde an der Stelle des ungeplanten Zwischenstopps auf dem Geinsheimer Kornsand ein schlichtes, aus Bruchsteinen massiv gefügtes Denkmal errichtet. Die Inschriftentafel auf der Mauer zwischen zwei Rundsäulen erinnert an das Ereignis.

On 4 August 1908, an engine defect forced the famous Count Ferdinand von Zeppelin (1838–1917) to make an emergency landing near Geinsheim am Rhein while on an endurance flight from Constance to Mainz. One year later, this was deemed reason enough to erect a monument commemorating both the event and the huge fascination held for the "giants of the air" during the imperial period.

Zeppelindenkmal
Kornsand
65468 Trebur
www.schloesser-hessen.de/
de/zeppelindenkmal

In 1900, Count Ferdinand von Zeppelin (1838–1917) made a breakthrough with his design for a rigid airship stabilised with a metal frame, a technology that was to revolutionise civil and military aviation. At the time, Zeppelins could fly higher and further than propeller aircraft, and carry heavier loads.

However, a mishap occurred in Geinsheim in southern Hesse on 4 August 1908 when the Count was forced to make an emergency landing with his LZ-4 airship on his first long-distance flight. Although he reached Mainz that same evening, he had to make a further unplanned stop on the return flight to Constance the following day. It was there that the airship broke away from its anchorage and burst into flames.

Just a year later a simple monument made of huge quarry stones was erected at the site of the unplanned stop on Kornsand in Geinsheim. The inscription plate positioned on the wall between two round pillars recalls the event.

UNESCO-WELTERBE OBERES MITTELRHEINTAL

UNESCO WORLD HERITAGE SITE "UPPER MIDDLE RHINE VALLEY"

BURGRUINE EHRENFELS, RÜDESHEIM AM RHEIN

EHRENFELS CASTLE RUINS, RÜDESHEIM AM RHEIN

Kurz hinter Rüdesheim knickt der Rhein scharf von seinem Lauf westwärts nach Norden ab. Dort liegt malerisch hoch über dem Fluss inmitten von Weinbergen die Burgruine Ehrenfels. Sie bildet den Eingang zum 67 Kilometer langen UNESCO-Welterbe Oberes Mittelrheintal, und damit den Auftakt zu einer Kette von Burgen, die diesen engen und wildromantischen Flussverlauf prägen.

Philipp von Bolanden (?–1220) errichtete die Hangburg zwischen 1208 und 1220. Erstmals urkundlich erwähnt wurde sie allerdings erst, als Philipps Witwe die Burg an das Erzbistum Mainz abtreten musste. In der Folge-

zeit verblieb die Anlage im Eigentum der Mainzer Erzbischöfe, die sie im 14. Jahrhundert erweiterten und als Residenz ausbauten.

Neben militärstrategischen Funktionen diente die Burg auch als Zollstation. Aufgrund ihrer Lage am Binger Loch, das Handelsschiffe nur langsam passieren konnten, war sie dafür gut geeignet. Im Verbund mit dem sogenannten Mäuseturm auf einer vorgelagerten Insel ließ sich der Fluss bequem überwachen. Die Anlage überstand den Dreißigjährigen Krieg (1618–1648), wurde aber im Pfälzischen Erbfolgekrieg (1688–1697) von französischen Truppen in Brand gesteckt und blieb seitdem Ruine.

Die trapezförmige Kernburg mit engem Hof hatte einen langgestreckten, dreistöckigen Palas zum Rhein hin, von dem sich Reste erhalten haben. Außerdem steht bis heute eine beeindruckende Schildmauer mit Wehrgängen und zwei runden Ecktürmen.

Just downstream of Rüdesheim, the River Rhine veers sharply from its westward course towards the north. It is here that the Ehrenfels Castle Ruins sit majestically among vineyards, high above the Rhine. They form the entrance to the 67-kilometre-long UNESCO World Heritage site known as the Upper Middle Rhine Valley, and thus the start of a series of castles that shape this narrow, wildly romantic river course.

Burgruine Ehrenfels
65385 Rüdesheim am Rhein
www.schloesser-hessen.de/
de/burgruine-ehrenfels

Philipp von Bolanden (?–1220) constructed the hillside castle between 1208 and 1220. However, the first documented mention of the castle was when Philipp's widow was forced to hand the castle over to the Archbishopric of Mainz. In the years that followed, the castle remained the property of the archbishops of Mainz, who expanded it and converted it into a residence in the 14th century.
In addition to strategic military functions, the castle also served as a toll station. Its position on the Binger Loch, which merchant ships could only pass slowly, made it ideal for this purpose. The river could *be easily monitored from the castle in connection with the Mouse Tower, sited on an offshore island. The complex survived the Thirty Years' War (1618–1648), but was set on fire by French soldiers during the Palatinate War of Succession (1688–1697) and has remained a ruin ever since.*
The trapezium-shaped central part of the castle with its narrow courtyard had a long, three-storey great hall overlooking the Rhine, of which some remains have been preserved. An impressive defensive wall with battlements and two round corner towers also remain standing today.

OSTEINSCHER NIEDERWALD, RÜDESHEIM AM RHEIN

OSTEIN'S NIEDERWALD PARK, RÜDESHEIM AM RHEIN

Der Osteinsche Niederwald liegt auf einem Plateau oberhalb von Rüdesheim. Die Gartenanlage aus dem 18. Jahrhundert orientierte sich an englischen Landschaftsgärten, die anders als die geometrischen Barockgärten Frankreichs einen natürlichen Landschaftseindruck evozieren sollten. Damals wie heute bezaubert die Verbindung der von kleinen Bauten belebten Parklandschaft mit herrlichen Ausblicken über den Rhein.

1763 hatte Graf Karl Maximilian von Ostein (1735–1809) das rund 304 Hektar große Areal geerbt und er verwandelte einen Teil davon über Jahrzehnte in einen Parkwald. Im Süden ließ er sich eine Sommerresidenz mitsamt repräsentativer Zufahrt und Wegenetz errichten. Den zum Zierwald umgewidmeten Teil ließ der Graf von forstlicher Nutzung und Viehmast ausnehmen und die Gehölze wild durchwachsen. Er setzte kleine Gebäudestaffagen hinein, die zusammen mit neuen Baumarten, Sträuchern und anderen Zierpflanzungen Raumbilder erschufen. So erinnerten eine künstliche Ruine, die Rossel, sowie ein Klippenhaus an das idealisierte Mittelalter. Besonders beeindruckend sind die abwechslungsreichen Aussichten auf das Rheintal, die bewusst in die Gesamtanlage einbezogen wurden. Reizvolle Fernblicke, die sich beim Durchstreifen des Parks immer wieder auftun, bringen diese einzigartige naturräumliche Situation zur Geltung.

◄ Der Monopteros mit dem Blick auf das Rheintal
The monopteros with view towards the Rhine Valley

▲ Die Ruine des neugotischen Rittersaals
The ruins of the neo-Gothic knights' hall

▶ Die Rossel, eine künstlich angelegte Ruine des Landschaftsgartens
The Rossel, an artificial ruin in the landscape garden

▼ Blick von der oberen Terrasse der Rossel auf Burg Ehrenfels, den Rhein mit dem Mäuseturm und den Fluss Nahe
View from the upper terrace towards the Rossel at castle ruins Ehrenfels, the River Rhine with the Mäuseturm and the River Nahe

Ostein's Niederwald Park sits on a plateau above Rüdesheim. Dating from the 18th century, the park was based on English landscape garden design, which, in contrast to the geometric Baroque gardens of France, was intended to evoke natural landscapes. Today as in the past, the site offers a magical blend of a park landscape dotted with small structures and magnificent views of the Rhine.

▼ Ein Leitsystem führt durch die Geschichte des Landschaftsgartens
Information signs guide visitors through the history of the landscape garden

▲ Blick auf den Park mit der über-
kuppelten Zauberhütte
*View of the park with the domed en-
chanted pavilion*

Osteinscher Niederwald
65385 Rüdesheim am Rhein
www.schloesser-hessen.de/
de/osteinscher-niederwald

*Count Karl Maximilian von Ostein
(1735–1809) inherited the area of around
304 hectares in 1763 and over a period of
decades, he transformed part of it into
a wooded park. He had a a summer residence built in the south part of the park,
including an impressive entrance and a
network of paths. He stopped the section
of the park that was devoted to an ornamental wood from being used for forestry
and animal husbandry, allowing the trees
and shrubs to grow wild. He added small
ornamental structures, which together
with new tree species, shrubs and other
ornamental plants, created "spatial pic-
tures". For example, an artificial ruin,
the Rossel, along with a cliff-top house,
are reminiscent of the idealised Middle
Ages.
The changing views over the Rhine Valley
are particularly impressive and were de-
liberately incorporated into the overall design. Multiple delightful distant views are
revealed to visitors as they stroll through
the park, accentuating its unique geo-
graphical position.*

NIEDERWALDDENKMAL, RÜDESHEIM AM RHEIN

NIEDERWALD MONUMENT, RÜDESHEIM AM RHEIN

In monumentalem Ausmaß erinnert das Niederwalddenkmal am Eingang zum UNESCO-Welterbe Oberes
Mittelrheintal an den Deutsch-Französischen Krieg
1870/71 und die Gründung des Deutschen Kaiserreiches.
Oberhalb von Rüdesheim am Rhein, an einem Standort
mit schöner Fernsicht, verherrlicht der Touristenmag-
net den Zusammenschluss von 25 Einzelstaaten und
Freien Städten aus einer preußischen idealisierenden
Perspektive.

Niederwalddenkmal
65385 Rüdesheim am Rhein
www.schloesser-hessen.de/
de/niederwalddenkmal

▲ Das Niederwalddenkmal erinnert an die Gründung des Deutschen Kaiserreiches nach dem Sieg über Frankreich 1870/71
The Niederwald Monument commemorates the founding of the German Empire after the victory over France in 1870/71

◄ Kaiser Wilhelm I. im Zentrum des Feldherrenreliefs
King William of Prussia, the future Emperor William I in the centre of the relief depicting army commanders

Im Jahr seiner Errichtung war das über 38 Meter hohe Niederwalddenkmal bei Rüdesheim am Rhein das bedeutendste Denkmalprojekt des Kaiserreiches. Finanziert aus Spenden und zu einem großen Teil mit Mitteln des Staates, wurde das dreiteilige Monument 1883 eingeweiht. Es besteht aus einem Unterbau, hohem Sockel und einer kolossalen bronzenen Germania-Statue, die die geeinte Nation verkörpert. Entworfen und ausgeführt hatten es der Bildhauer Johannes Schilling (1828–1910) und der Architekt Karl Weißbach (1841–1905) mit einem ausführlichen und spannungsreichen Bild- und Textprogramm. Das Standbild, die Reliefs, Symbole, Wappen und allegorischen Figuren erzählen vom Auszug in den Krieg, dem Sieg über die Franzosen und der dadurch ermöglichten Bildung des ersten deutschen Nationalstaates. Unverhohlen setzt das Niederwalddenkmal Preußens Führungsrolle in Szene. Zudem vermittelt es eine die Tatsachen verdrehende Sinnstiftung des mit inneren Schwierigkeiten gestarteten Kaiserreiches. Unwahr ist die Behauptung der zentralen Inschrift, die neu geschaffene Hohenzollern-Erbmonarchie beerbe das 1806 untergegangene Heilige Römische Reich Deutscher Nation. So steht das Denkmal letztlich auch für preußische Geschichtspolitik.

With its bombastic proportions, the Niederwald Monument at the gateway to the UNESCO World Heritage Site Upper Middle Rhine Valley commemorates the Franco-Prussian War of 1870/1871 and the founding of the German Empire. Overlooking Rüdesheim am Rhein from a vantage offering expansive views, this tourist magnet commemorates the fusion of 25 separate states and free cities from an idealising Prussian perspective.

▲ Blick über die Germania
in das Rheintal
*View over the Germania Statue
into the Rhine Valley*

In the year of its erection, the 38-metre-tall Niederwald Monument in Rüdesheim am Rhein was the Empire's most significant monument project. Financed from donations and to a large part through public funds, the three-part monument was dedicated in 1883. It consists of a base, a high plinth and an enormous bronze statue of Germania that embodies the unified nation. It was designed and created by the sculptor Johannes Schilling (1828–1910) and by the architect Karl Weißbach (1841–1905) and includes an extensive and fascinating series of images and texts. The statue, reliefs, symbols, coats of arms and allegorical figures recount going to war, the victory over France and the formation of the first German nation state made possible as a result. The Niederwald Monument unashamedly spotlights Prussia's leadership role. It also portrays a distorted view of the facts by giving a sense of the empire being established at a time of internal difficulties. The claim set out in the central inscription that the newly created hereditary monarchy of the Hohenzollerns is the heir to the Holy Roman Empire of the German Nation, which was eliminated in 1806, is untrue. The monument thus ultimately also stands for Prussian historical policy.

VOM ODENWALD ZUM NECKAR

FROM THE ODENWALD FOREST TO THE NECKAR RIVER

SCHLOSS ERBACH
ERBACH PALACE

Schloss Erbach im Odenwald verdankt seine Schätze
vor allem der Sammelleidenschaft des Grafen Franz I.
zu Erbach-Erbach (1754–1823). Er war hochgebildet und
stand in Kontakt mit vielen Geistesgrößen seiner Zeit.
Seine reichen Kunstsammlungen sollten Geschichte
bewahren und gleichzeitig für die Zukunft erfahrbar
machen.

Schloss Erbach
Marktplatz 7
64711 Erbach
www.schloesser-hessen.de/
de/schloss-erbach

1736 bauten die Grafen von Erbach ihre Residenz in eine repräsentative Barockanlage um. Zu überregionalem Ruhm aber gelangte das Schloss erst durch Graf Franz, der hier seine beeindruckenden Sammlungen aufbewahrte und präsentierte. 1791 gelang ihm auf einer Italienreise der Ankauf einer Antikensammlung. Für diese Objekte ließ er eigens drei Zimmer im Schloss gestalten, die er „meine Wohnzimmer" nannte, darunter ein Etruskisches Kabinett.

Neben Objekten der Antike sammelte der Graf auch Waffen, Rüstungen, Glasmalereien sowie Geweihe, die bis heute im neogotischen Rittersaal und der sogenannten Gewehrkammer prä-

sentiert werden. Auch seine Vorliebe für die Elfenbeinschnitzerei, die in Erbach einen ganzen Handwerkszweig erblühen ließ, ist im Schloss nachvollziehbar, wo das Deutsche Elfenbeinmuseum Objekte aus drei Jahrhunderten präsentiert.

Der Enkel von Franz, Graf Eberhard XV. (1818–1884), baute die Sammlung seines Großvaters aus und erweiterte sie um neue Sammelgebiete, so etwa die sakrale Kunst, für die er einen „Heiligthumsraum" im Schloss einrichtete. Sein prominentestes Stück: der Schöllenbacher Altar, ein spätgotisches Schnitzretabel mit einer Wurzel-Jesse-Darstellung.

▼ Audienzzimmer des Grafen Franz I.
zu Erbach-Erbach (1754–1823)
Audience chamber of Count Franz I zu
Erbach-Erbach (1754–1823)

▲ Die Hirschgalerie
The deer gallery

▲ Die Sammlung mittelalterlicher
Waffen und Rüstungen, die Graf
Franz I. schon in den 1780er Jahren
begann, ist eine der frühesten der-
artiger Sammlungen in Deutschland
*The collection of medieval weapons
and suits of armour started by Count
Franz I as early as the 1780s is one
of the earliest such collections in
Germany*

Above all else, Erbach Palace in the Odenwald Forest owes its treasures to the passion for collecting developed by Count Franz I of Erbach-Erbach (1754–1823). A highly learned man, he was in contact with numerous great thinkers of his era. In assembling his collections he sought to preserve history while making it tangible for the future.

In 1736 the Counts of Erbach remodelled their residence to create a prestigious Baroque complex. However, it only acquired supra-regional fame through Count Franz, who kept and presented his impressive collections at the castle. In 1791 he purchased a collection of antiques while travelling in Italy. He created additional three rooms in the palace for these objects, which he lovingly referred to as "my living rooms", and which included an Etruscan closet.

In addition to antique objects, the Count also collected weapons, suits of armour, glass paintings and antlers, which are to-day still presented in a neo-Gothic knights' hall and a rifle chamber. His love of ivory carvings, which led to an entire branch of handicraft evolving in Erbach, is also evident in the palace, where the German Ivory Museum presents items spanning three centuries.

Franz's grandson, Count Eberhard XV (1818–1884), continued to develop his grandfather's collection and extended it to include new subject areas such as sacred art, for which he built a "sanctuary room" within the palace. His most prominent piece is the Schöllenbach Altar, a late-Gothic carved retabula depicting Jesse's Root.

▼ Der Oraniersaal
The Orange Hall

188

▲ Der 1515 fertiggestellte
Schöllenbacher Altar
The Schöllenbach Altar,
completed in 1515

▶ Aus der Porzellansammlung
der Grafen zu Erbach
Items from Erbach's porcelain
collection

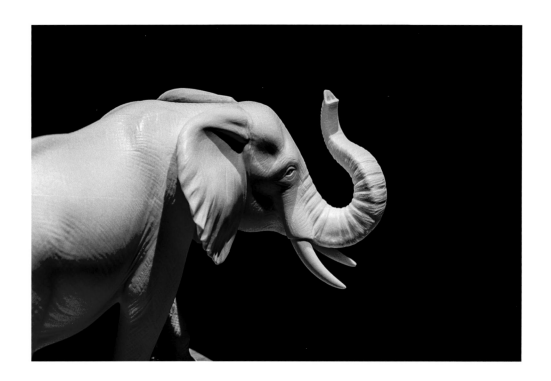

▲ Rudolf Schwinn (geb. 1940),
Elefant, zweite Hälfte des 20. Jahrhunderts, Deutsches Elfenbeinmuseum Schloss Erbach
*Rudolf Schwinn (born 1940), Elephant,
second half of the 20th century,
German Ivory Museum, Erbach Palace*

◄ Ferdinand Preiss (1882–1943),
Iphigenie, 1920er Jahre oder früher,
Deutsches Elfenbeinmuseum Schloss
Erbach
*Ferdinand Preiss (1882–1943), Iphi-
genie, 1920s or earlier, German Ivory
Museum, Erbach Palace*

◄ ▲ ▶ Impression aus dem
Deutschen Elfenbeinmuseum
*Images from the German Ivory
Museum*

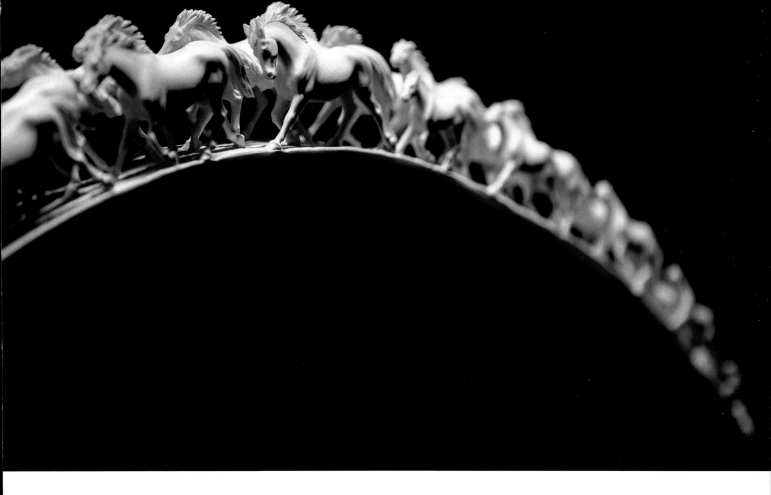

▲ Rudolf Schwinn (geb. 1940),
Pferdebrücke, zweite Hälfte des
20. Jahrhunderts, Deutsches Elfenbeinmuseum Schloss Erbach
*Rudolf Schwinn (born 1940), Horse
bridge, second half of the 20th century,
German Ivory Museum, Erbach Palace*

▶ Der große Vitrinenraum des
Deutschen Elfenbeinmuseums zeigt
Elfenbeinwerke Graf Franz' I.
*The large display area of the German
Ivory Museum shows ivory works of
Count Franz I*

SCHLOSS LICHTENBERG

LICHTENBERG PALACE

Eindrucksvoll erhebt sich Schloss Lichtenberg auf einem
Bergkegel in der malerischen Odenwaldlandschaft.
Die dreiflügelige Anlage, die als das erste Renaissance-
schloss Hessens gilt, wurde als Sommerresidenz der
Landgrafen von Hessen-Darmstadt errichtet. Sie diente
als architektonisches Vorbild für weitere Bauten in der
Region.

Schloss Lichtenberg
64405 Fischbachtal-
Lichtenberg
www.schloesser-hessen.de/
de/schloss-lichtenberg

Die Grafen von Katzenelnbogen errichteten sich zu Beginn des 13. Jahrhunderts auf dem unbewaldeten, also ‚lichten‘ Hügel eine Burg. 1479 fiel die Anlage an die Landgrafen von Hessen. Georg I. (1547–1596) von Hessen-Darmstadt ließ sie zwischen 1570 und 1581 im Stil der Renaissance um- und ausbauen.

Heute weist die Anlage drei Flügel mit jeweils drei Geschossen auf. An der Fassade fallen die für die Renaissance typischen abgestuften und geschwungenen Giebel sowie die regelmäßige Reihung der Fenster auf. An der Nordseite hatte man als vierten Flügel den Katzenelnbogener Bau beibehalten, der jedoch im 19. Jahrhundert einstürzte und abgetragen wurde.

An Georg I. und seine erste Gemahlin Magdalena zur Lippe (1552–1587) erinnert das wappenbekrönte Portal des Ostflügels. Die Landgrafen nutzten Lichtenberg als Sommerresidenz sowie zur Zeit des Dreißigjährigen Krieges (1618–1648) mitunter als dauerhaften Wohnsitz. Ein wunderbarer Blick auf das Schloss bietet sich vom Anfang des 16. Jahrhunderts errichteten Bollwerk aus, das heute mitten im Ort Lichtenberg steht.

Lichtenberg Palace rises impressively on a hilltop within the picturesque Odenwald Forest landscape. The three-winged complex was the first Renaissance palace in Hesse and was built as a summer residence for the landgraves of Hesse-Darmstadt. It served as an architectural model for other buildings in the region.

◄ Das Innere des Geschützturms
The interior of the turret

▶ Trauzimmer im Südflügel
Wedding chamber in the south wing

▼ Wappenschilde der Landgrafschaft Hessen und der Grafschaft Katzenelnbogen
Coats of arms of the landgraviate of Hesse and of the county of Katzenelnbogen

At the beginning of the 13th century, the Counts of Katzenelnbogen built themselves a castle on the unforested (and therefore "light") hill. The castle's name is thus derived from the German word for light, "Licht". In 1479 the complex fell to the landgraves of Hesse. Georg I (1547–1596) of Hesse-Darmstadt had it modified and extended in the Renaissance style betweeen 1570 and 1581.

Today, the complex has three wings, each with three floors. The graduated curved gables typical of the Renaissance period are a striking feature of the façade, as is the arrangement of the windows in regular rows. A fourth wing of the Katzenelnbogen structure was retained on the north side, but this was removed after it collapsed in the 19th century.

The east wing's portal with its coats of arms commemorates George I and his wife, Magdalena zur Lippe (1552–1587). The landgraves used Lichtenberg as a summer residence and also occasionally as a primary residence during the Thirty Years' War (1618–1648). The bulwark, which was built from the beginning of the 16th century and which today stands in the centre of Lichtenberg, offers a wonderful view of the palace.

BURG BREUBERG

BREUBERG CASTLE

Burg Breuberg erhebt sich über dem Tal der Mümling im Vorderen Odenwald. Besucht man den Ort, so kann man die Geschichte der Burgenbaukunst zwischen dem 12. und dem 17. Jahrhundert am Objekt erleben, denn die Anlage wurde nie zerstört und war fast durchgängig bewohnt. So gehört sie heute zu den am besten erhaltenen Burgen im süddeutschen Raum.

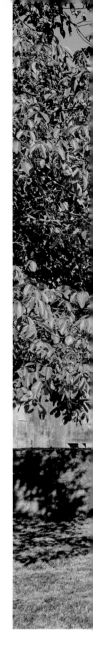

Blick auf die Vorburg mit dem Löwensteiner Kanzleibau
View to the outer bailey with the Löwenstein Wing.

◄ Kapelle
Chapel

Burg Breuberg
Burgstraße
65747 Breuberg
www.schloesser-hessen.de/
de/burg-breuberg

Von den Anfängen der Burg im 12. Jahrhundert zeugen noch der mächtige Bergfried aus Buckelquadern und das romanische Tor sowie die Ringmauer der Kernburg – als typische Elemente einer Burg der Stauferzeit. Die Herren von Breuberg und Erbauer der Anlage starben 1323 im Mannesstamm aus, woraufhin vier Adelsgeschlechter ihr Erbe antraten: Breuberg wurde zu einer sogenannten Ganerbenburg mit vertraglicher Regelung der Besitzverhältnisse und des gemeinsamen Lehens.

Eine der vier Familien, die Grafen von Wertheim, brachte die Burg schließlich ganz in ihren Besitz und baute sie ab dem ausgehenden 15. Jahrhundert zur Festung aus – die Erfindung der Feuerwaffen verlangten entsprechende Verteidigungsanlagen. Weitere Bautätigkeit erfolgte im 16. und 17. Jahrhundert unter den Grafen von Erbach und den Grafen von Löwenstein-Wertheim, die jetzt insbesondere Wert auf Wohnlichkeit und Repräsentation legten. Ganz im Stil der Renaissance zeigt sich der Anfang des 17. Jahrhunderts errichtete Johann-Casimir-Bau mit einer prachtvollen Stuckdecke.

Breuberg Castle rises above the Mümling Valley in the anterior Odenwald Forest region. Visitors to the site can experience for themselves the history of castle construction between the 12th and 17th centuries, as the castle was never destroyed and was inhabited almost continuously. This makes it one of the best-preserved castles in southern Germany today.

The mighty keep built of humpback stone blocks, the Romanesque gate and the curtain wall of the central part of the castle bear witness to the castle's beginnings in the 12th century and represent typical elements of a castle in the Staufen period. The male line of the Lords of Breuberg and original builders of the complex died out in 1323, at which time the castle was inherited by four noble families. Breuberg thus became a "Ganerbenburg", with its ownership status and joint occupancy regulated by means of a contract.

One of the four families, the Counts of Wertheim, finally brought the castle into its sole ownership. They expanded Breuberg into a fortress from the end of the 15th century as the advent of firearms called for corresponding defence installations. Further building activity followed in the 16th and 17th centuries under the Counts of Erbach and the Counts of Löwenstein-Wertheim, who now attached great importance to comfort and representation. The Johann-Casimir Building with its magnificent stuccoed ceiling was erected at the beginning of the 17th century and is very typical of the Renaissance style.

VESTE OTZBERG

OTZBERG FORTRESS

Der Basaltkegel, auf dem die am Rand des Odenwalds gelegene Veste Otzberg thront, ragt aus der Ebene empor. Vor allem der gedrungene, sich nach oben verjüngende Bergfried fällt auf – seine eigenartige Form hat ihm zusammen mit dem hellen Anstrich im Volksmund den Namen „Weiße Rübe" eingebracht. Vom Turm aus bietet sich ein herrlicher Blick, der an klaren Tagen bis nach Frankfurt reicht.

Veste Otzberg
Burgweg 28
64853 Otzberg
www.schloesser-hessen.de/
de/veste-otzberg

Knapp 25 Kilometer südöstlich von Darmstadt liegt die 1231 urkundlich erstmals erwähnte Veste Otzberg. Die Reichsabtei Fulda, der das Territorium um den Otzberg schon seit dem 8. Jahrhundert gehörte, hatte die Anlage nach 1220 errichten lassen. In den folgenden Jahrhunderten wechselte die Burg mehrfach die Besitzer. Sie war von Burgmannen besetzt, die von der jeweiligen Herrschaft mit ihrer Sicherung und Verteidigung betraut waren.

Charakteristisch für den Bau ist der ovale Grundriss, welcher der Form des Berges entspricht und durch die doppelten Ringmauern betont wird. Der Bergfried ist heute das einzige Gebäude, das noch aus dem 13. Jahrhundert stammt. Anfang des 16. Jahrhunderts wurde die innere Mauer verstärkt: Ein Wappen des Pfalzgrafen bei Rhein an ihrer Nordseite trägt die Jahreszahl 1518. 1574 entstanden das Kommandantenhaus sowie um 1600 die äußere Ringmauer.

Trotz ihrer Wehrhaftigkeit konnte die Festung der Belagerung im Dreißigjährigen Krieg (1618–1648) nicht standhalten, ihre Besatzung kapitulierte 1622. Ab 1803 gehörte die Veste endgültig zu Hessen-Darmstadt, ihre Gebäude dienten als Kaserne und Staatsgefängnis. 1826 wurden zahlreiche Bauten abgebrochen, und die Festung verfiel.

Otzberg Fortress sits majestically on a basalt hill that rises up from the plain on the edge of the Odenwald Forest. The stout keep that narrows towards the top is particularly striking – its unique shape combined with the light colour has led to it being referred to locally as the "White Turnip". The tower offers wonderful views extending as far as Frankfurt on clear days.

Otzberg Fortress, first mentioned in records in 1231, lies just under 25 kilometres south-east of Darmstadt. The Imperial Abbey of Fulda, to which the territory around Otzberg had belonged since the 8th century, had the complex constructed after 1220. In the centuries that followed, the castle saw several changes of ownership. It was occupied by knightly militia ("Burgmannen"), who were entrusted by the respective rulers to secure and defend the complex.

The oval layout, which reflects the shape of the hill and which is accentuated by the double curtain walls, is a characteristic feature of the structure. The keep is today the only surviving building from the 13th century. The inner wall was strengthened at the beginning of the 16th century. On its northern side, a coat of arms of the Counts Palatinate of the Rhine bears the date 1518. The commander's house was built in 1574 and the outer curtain wall around 1600.

Despite its defensive strength, the fortress was unable to withstand besiegement during the Thirty Years' War (1618–1648) and its garrison surrendered in 1622. From 1803 the fortress finally came into the hands of Hesse-Darmstadt, when its buildings served as barracks and as a state prison. In 1826, numerous buildings were demolished and the fortress fell into disrepair.

BURG HIRSCHHORN

HIRSCHHORN CASTLE

Ein Bergrücken zwischen Neckar- und Finkenbachtal
erschien den Herren von Hirschhorn als idealer
Ort für ihre Burg. Die Anlage, deren älteste Teile fast
800 Jahre alt sind, gehört mit ihrer unverwechselbaren
Silhouette aus Mauern, Giebeln und Turm heute zu
den schönsten im Neckartal – auch weil sie von größe-
ren Zerstörungen verschont blieb.

◀ Vorburg mit Stallbau und
Torhaus
*Castle's foreyard with stable and
gatehouse building*

Burg Hirschhorn
69434 Hirschhorn
www.schloesser-hessen.de/
de/burg-hirschhorn

Die weitläufige Burganlage besteht aus oberer und unterer Vorburg sowie der vergleichsweise engen Kernburg, zu welcher der Bergfried, einige Wohn- und Wirtschaftsgebäude sowie eine gewaltige Schildmauer gehören. Errichtet in der Mitte des 13. Jahrhunderts, erfolgte bereits im 14. Jahrhundert ein erster Ausbau. Die Herren von Hirschhorn waren gut betucht: Sie verfügten über umfangreiche Besitzungen und einflussreiche Ämter am Hofe des pfälzischen Kurfürsten.

Hirschhorn war, wie die meisten Burgen der Zeit, ein eigener kleiner Kosmos. Neben den Rittern und ihren Familien wohnten auch Tor- und Turmwächter, Jäger, Stallknechte, Hirten, Mägde, Dienerinnen, Burgverwalter und ein Geistlicher auf der Burg. Außer den Wohngebäuden gab es Marstall, Ställe und Scheune (heute zum Teil erhalten) sowie weitere Wirtschaftsgebäude, die sich nicht erhalten haben.

Mit den Erweiterungen des 16. Jahrhunderts gaben die Hirschhorner ihrer Burg den Charakter eines repräsentativen Schlosses. Sie ließen zum Neckar hin einen Garten anlegen und einen prächtigen Renaissancebau errichten, den sogenannten Hatzfeldbau.

◀ Mittelalterlicher Palas
Medieval great hall

The Lords of Hirschhorn decided that the ridge of a hill between the Neckar and Finkenbach valleys was the perfect place for their castle. With its unmistakable silhouette of walls, gables and tower, the complex, whose oldest parts date back almost 800 years, is today one of the most attractive in the Neckar Valley – not least because it has escaped major destruction.

▶ Innenraum im renaissance-zeitlichen Hatzfeldbau
Renaissance room in the Hatzfeld Wing

▲ Ansicht von Nordwesten
zu Wehranlage, Bergfried und
Zugangstor
*View from northwest to the
fortifications, the keep and the
main gate*

The extensive castle complex comprises an upper and lower outer bailey with a comparatively narrow central part which includes the keep, some residential and farm buildings and a mighty defensive wall. Built in the middle of the 13th century, the castle underwent a first extension as soon as the 14th century. The Lords of Hirschhorn were very wealthy, having many possessions and influential offices at the court of the Palatinate Electoral Princes.

Like most castles of its time, Hirschhorn formed its own small cosmos. In addition to the knights and their families, the castle was also inhabited by gatekeepers and tower guardians, hunters, grooms, shepherds, maidservants, maids, castle stewards and a clergyman. In addition to the residential buildings, the complex also included stables, cowsheds and a barn (some of which are still standing today) as well as other farm buildings which have not been preserved.

The 16th-century extensions gave the Hirschhorn family a castle with the character of a representative palace. They created a garden extending towards the Neckar River and constructed a splendid Renaissance structure known as the Hatzfeld Building.

IMPRESSUM / LEGAL NOTICE

Herausgeber / *Publisher*
Staatliche Schlösser und Gärten Hessen /
State Palaces and Gardens Hesse

Direktorin / *Director*
Kirsten Worms

Fotos / *Photographs*
Michael Leukel

Konzeption und Schriftleitung /
Design and editorship
Dr. Katharina Bechler

Katalog- und Bildredaktion /
Catalogue and image editing
Esther Walldorf M. A.

Texte / *Texts*
Dr. Claudia Caesar
Dr. Susanne Király
Katharina Saul M. A.
Elisabeth Weymann M. A.

Bauhistorische Beratung /
Architectural heritage consultancy
Dr. Anja Dötsch

Gartenhistorische Beratung /
Garden history consultancy
Dr. Inken Formann

Übersetzung / *Translation*
HIGH-TECH Hay GmbH

Lektorat / *Editors*
Thomas Aufleger M. A.
Dorothée Baganz M. A., Michael Imhof Verlag

Reproduktion und Gestaltung /
Reproduction and design
Vicki Schirdewahn, Michael Imhof Verlag

Druck und Bindung / *Printing and binding*
Grafisches Centrum Cuno, Calbe

© 2021
Michael Imhof Verlag GmbH & Co. KG,
Michael Leukel und Autoren / *and authors*

Michael Imhof Verlag GmbH & Co. KG
Stettiner Straße 25
D-36100 Petersberg
Tel. 0661 / 29 19 166-0
Fax 0661 / 29 19 166-9
info@imhof-verlag.de
www.imhof-verlag.de

Printed in Germany

ISBN 978-3-7319-1126-5

HESSEN

Staatliche
Schlösser und Gärten
Hessen

Bilder Einband:
Arkadenbau und Kavaliersbau im Staatspark
Hanau-Wilhelmsbad (Vorderseite),
Burgruine Ehrenfels (Rückseite)

Cover images:
Hanau-Wilhelmsbad, arcade building and cavalry
building in the Wilhelmsbad State Park (front page),
Ehrenfels Castle Ruins (back page)

Einbandinnenseite:
Schloss Weilburg, Pariser Zimmer (vorne),
Schloss Bad Homburg, Königsflügel, Boisiertes
Kabinett (hinten)

Inside cover:
Weilburg Palace, Parisian room (front),
Bad Homburg Palace, King's Wing, wood-panelled
room (back)

Porträtfotos / *portraits*:
S./p. 10: Hessische Staatskanzlei
S./p. 12: kunst.hessen.de
S./p. 14: Staatliche Schlösser und Gärten Hessen,
Foto: Alexander Paul Englert
S./p. 18: Anja Leukel

Schmuckseiten:
S. 2: Schmuckportal mit Landgraf Friedrich II.,
Schloss Bad Homburg
S. 4/5: Schloss Erbach, Deutsches Elfenbein-
museum, Elefant von Rudolf Schwinn – Elisabeth-
brunnen Marburg-Schröck – Kloster Seligenstadt,
Prälatur – Burgruine Ehrenfels – Schloss Weilburg,
Kurfürstliches Gemach – Niederwalddenkmal
S. 6/7: Schloss Erbach – Schloss Bad Homburg,
Herkules im Königsflügel – Prinz-Georg-Garten,
Darmstadt – Brentanohaus, Roter Salon, Oestrich-
Winkel – Propstei Fulda, nordöstliches Eckzimmer –
Fürstengruft Butzbach
S. 8/9: Schlosspark Bad Homburg mit dem Weißen
Turm und der Romanischen Halle
S. 16/17: Das Untere Parterre im Schlosspark Weil-
burg
S. 206/207: Burg Hirschhorn

Decorative pages:
p. 2: Decorative portal depicting Landgrave Fried-
rich II, Bad Homburg Palace
p. 4/5: Erbach Palace, German Ivory Museum,
Elephant by Rudolf Schwinn – Elisabeth Fountain
Marburg-Schröck – Seligenstadt Abbey, Prelature –
Ehrenfels Castle Ruins – Weilburg Palace, Elector's
Chamber – Niederwald Monument
p. 6/7: Erbach Palace – Bad Homburg Palace,
Hercules in the King's Wing – Prince George Garden,
Darmstadt – Brentano House, Red Room, Oestrich-
Winkel – Provostry Buildings Fulda, northeastern
corner room, ceiling fresco – The Fürstengruft
Princely Crypt Butzbach
p. 8/9: Bad Homburg Palace Park with the White
Tower and the Romanesque Hall
p. 16/17: The lower parterre in Weilburg Palace
Park
p. 206/207: Hirschhorn Castle